Easy Origami

MW01169176

Easy Origami

Origami is fun and good for you! The traditional Japanese art of paper folding is presented in this book that is easy for everyone to understand and follow. The combination of step-by-step instructions, clear diagrams, and explanatory videos makes it especially easy to follow along.

The book contains 30 models, ranging from simple to challenging. This guarantees folding fun for beginners, and advanced folders can take on exciting challenges.

Simple and easy-to-understand instructions

Good, easy-to-follow instructions with logically sequenced stages are the key to blissful folding fun. Our tried and tested step-by-step folding instructions are clear, well laid out and are complemented by descriptive diagrams. They are structured in such a way that even children and origami beginners can easily understand and follow them. And if you get stuck despite all this, our explanatory videos will help you.

Individual support through video explanations

Each individual instruction is supplemented by an explanatory video in which the individual folding steps are shown to you slowly and memorably. It can be accessed via a QR code. Especially for more complex objects, a video showing the individual folds is very helpful.

Three difficulty levels

Different levels of difficulty provide varied folding fun for beginners, intermediate and expert folders. Each instruction is marked with one, two or three stars, so you can find the project that suits you at a glance. The complexity of an object results not only from the number of folds, but also from the demands made on concentration, spatial imagination and fine motor skills. For beginners, we recommend starting with the first object and then slowly working your way up to the more complex models. You will notice that you gain skill and dexterity after a short time.

Getting started

Beginner ★ ★ ★

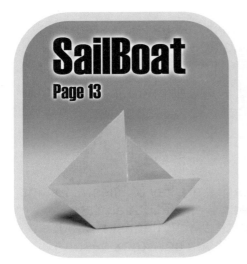

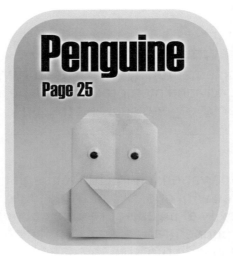

Beginner ★ ☆ ☆

Rectangular Box

Crown

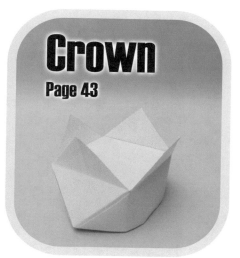

Bat

Bee

Fish

Elephant Head

Medium

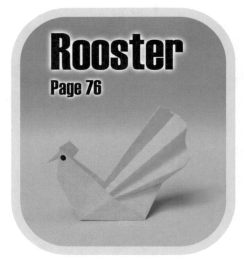

Expert ★★★

Cow
Page 85

Squid
Page 88

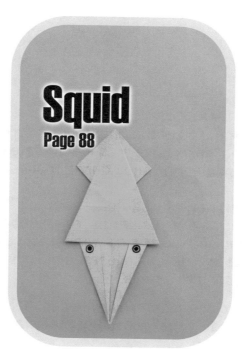

Grasshoper
Page 91

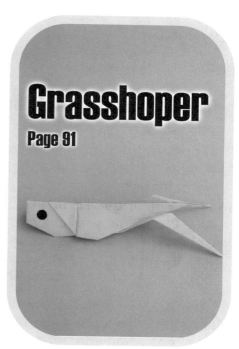

Crane
Page 94

Frog
Page 97

Turtle
Page 100

Origami Fun

The art of paper folding

Origami is a Japanese word composed of the components "oru" – to fold and "kami" – paper. However, the term "paper folding" only conveys an incomplete idea of the essence of this art, in which dexterity, relaxation, imagination and educational benefits form a unique combination.
In Japan, origami is an important part of traditional culture. The creative hobby has now also found many followers in Germany. In kindergartens, schools, therapeutic institutions or at home - origami inspires young and old. It's no wonder, because the art of folding imaginative figures out of paper is fun, can be learned quickly, promotes dexterity and concentration and many other cognitive skills.

The figures range from simple to complex. While you can make simple objects with five to six folds, there are also many models that consist of many folding steps and require time, concentration and patience to make.

The great thing about origami is that kindergarten children enjoy creative folding just as much as grandma and grandpa, beginners enjoy quick successes and advanced students enjoy exciting challenges.

Getting started in the wonderful world of origami is quite uncomplicated. All you need is a sheet of paper, your fingers and a little patience. Scissors or glue are not necessary.

Have fun!

Origami History

Paper and the origins of origami

The search for the origins of origami takes us to China. The technique of making paper was discovered there around the year 100 BC. To make it, people mixed finely chopped mulberry bark, shredded rags and hemp, and added water. The resulting mass was pressed flat, the liquid was squeezed out and everything was left to dry in the sun. This method of papermaking was comparatively simple and inexpensive!

Buddhist monks brought paper and the secret of its production to Japan in the sixth and seventh centuries. In its early days, it was considered a precious treasure used exclusively in religious ceremonies. Even today, white strips of paper folded in a zigzag shape are used in Shinto rituals.

During the Edo period (1603 - 1867), Japan experienced a period of peace, political stability and economic prosperity. Paper became a commonly available and frequently used commodity. It was also during this time that the tradition of folding paper according to patterns passed down from generation to generation. It was also given as an offering or as a greeting card along with gifts.

Origami becomes increasingly popular

Thus, origami became more and more popular. People discovered origami as a creative, useful and relaxing pastime. They made small objects as gifts or as decoration for their homes. This period also saw the emergence of the classic basic shapes. These include the frog, the swan or the crane. In 1797, "Senbazuru" was published, the first book on paper folding in general and specifically on the folding of cranes. The crane is considered a symbol of good luck in Japan. Even today, on special occasions, birthdays or weddings, people give a folded paper crane as a gift. Anyone who folds 1000 origami cranes will have a wish granted by the gods - at least that's what an old legend says.

Origami today

The worldwide origami frenzy is also due to the works of Akira Yoshizawa (1911 - 2005). The "father of modern origami" is said to have developed over 50,000 origami models in his lifetime. He created new techniques and shapes and invented a system of simple, easy-to-understand drawings, dotted and dashed lines, and other symbols to represent the folding process. This system was then expanded upon by American origami artist Samuel Randlett. The merits of the Yoshizawa-Randlett system were obvious and were quickly taken up by the international origami society. The system is the basis for folding instructions that enthusiasts all over the world can use to recreate the various patterns.

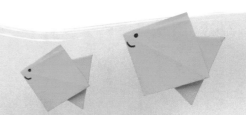

Basic folds and shapes

The foundation of any origami piece, no matter how complex, is two simple folds – isn't that fascinating? In the valley fold, the paper is folded upwards along an imaginary line so that a valley is formed in the middle. In the instructions, the valley fold is indicated by a dashed black line. The mountain fold is the counterpart, so to speak, because the paper is folded backwards so that a mountain is formed. The mountain fold is indicated in the instructions by a dot-dash line.

These folds are the foundation for various basic shapes. The classic basic shapes include:

- the blintz fold
- the Dragon
- the bird
- the fish
- the water bomb

Most of the countless origami models are created from these basic shapes. For example, the Blintz shape is the basis for the decorative water lily, the bird shape gives rise to the famous crane, and the dragon shape becomes an elegant swan in the blink of an eye after just a few folds.

Once you discover the creative possibilities that lie in a simple paper square, you will quickly fall in love with this great hobby.

The right paper

In order for you to enjoy stunning results when folding, it is important to use the right paper. It should be strong, but also flexible and easy to fold without the color flaking off. A variety of high-quality origami papers are available in stores in a wide range of sizes, patterns and colors. Standard sizes are sheets with side length 7.5 cm, 15 cm, 18 cm, 20 cm and 25 cm. Beginners and little kids can start with a 25 x 25 cm sheet and then slowly move on to smaller sizes. The thickness is usually between 60 and 90 g/m^2. The thinner the paper, the easier it is to fold; thicker paper produces a more robust result. Here you have to try out which size and thickness is optimal for your individual project.

Furthermore, you have the choice between solid-colored paper, which has the same color on both sides, and paper where the front and back sides have different colors. With this paper you can achieve fascinating effects, on the other hand there are also projects where monochrome paper is ideal.

Washi or Japanese paper is a particularly noble, handmade paper. It is characterized by its firm, cloth-like structure, softness and stability. The paper is obtained from the fibers of plants and shrubs native to Japan and its production is very complex. No wonder such a high-quality product is expensive! Before you fold a figure from Japanese paper, you should first practice a little with cheaper paper – later you can always fall back on the noble Washi.

Flip Model

Turn the whole model over so that the underside now faces you. Origami Paper is coloured on one side, white on the other side.

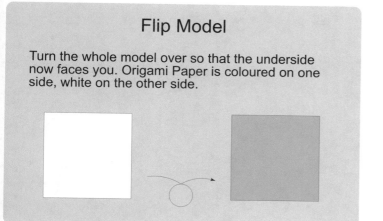

Rotate Mode

Turn the model while keeping the same side facing you. The angle of rotation is shown inside the symbol.

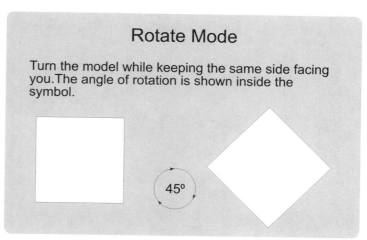

Valley fold

Fold the paper towards yourself along the dashed line

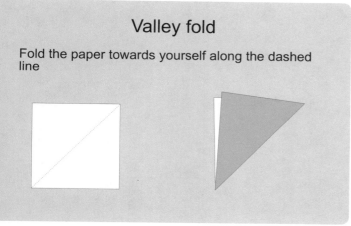

Mountain fold

Fold the paper away from yourself (underneath) along the dashed line.

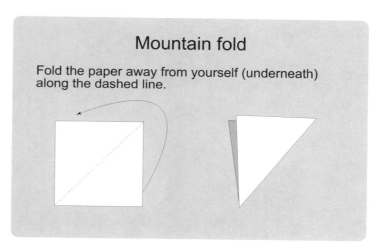

Fold and Unfold (Crease)

Make a fold (valley or mountain as indicated by the line style) and then unfold to leave a crease line.

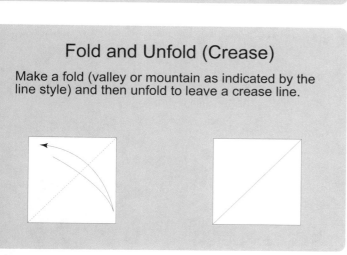

Repeat behind

Perform the same step on the underside of the model. The number of bars across the arrow indicates the number of times to repeat the steps. In this case, once

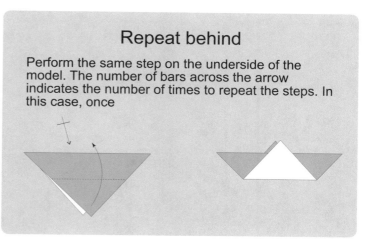

Inflate

Blow into the hole in the model where shown to inflate it.

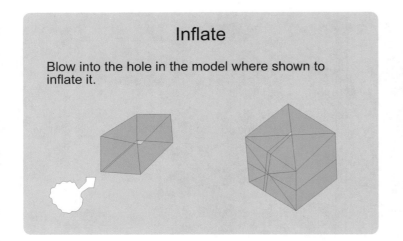

Sink or Push in

Push part of the model back in on itself so that valleys become mountains and vice versa It helps to crease before making the sink.

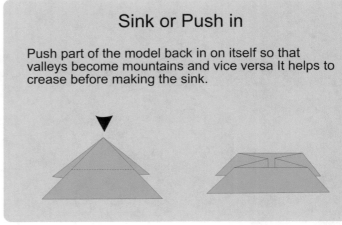

Pull out

Pull where shown, to extend a flap move part of the model, or similar.

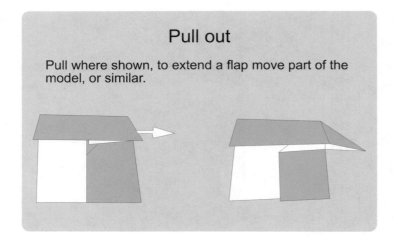

Pleat fold

Alternative mountain and valley folds to create a pleat, or concertina pattern.

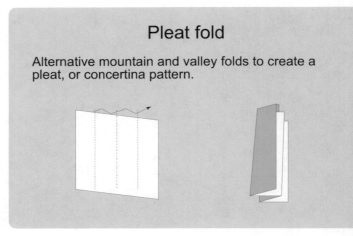

Inside reverse fold

Push the tip down between the layers on the open side reversing it so that itsmountain becomes a valley. It helps to crease before making fold.

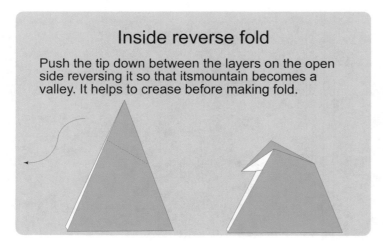

Outside reverse fold

Pull the tip across the closed side. The model will need to open up slightly as the reverse takes place. It helps to crease before making fold.

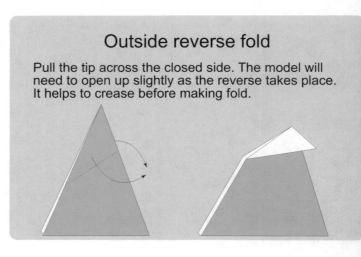

Squash fold

The Diagram

First crease the valley

Pull the tip over bending the paper

Press flat forming the mountain in the diagram.

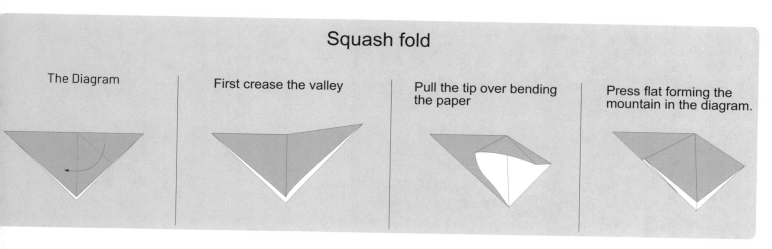

Petal fold

The Diagram

First crease all the folds as valley

Lift the top layer and reverse the top layer creases to make them into mountain

Keep lifting, the sides will fold in

Press flat

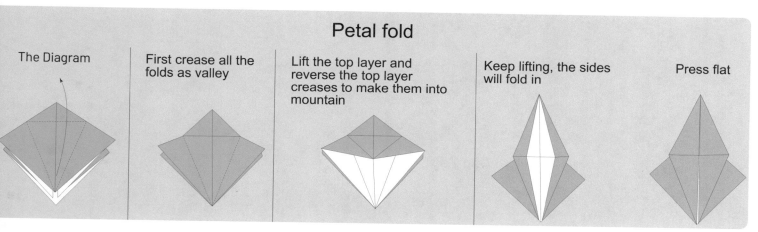

Rabbit (or Rabbit ear) fold

The Diagram

First crease valley These will all be angle bisector

Close all three at once bending the paper between

Press the new flap down flat, forming the mountain in the diagram

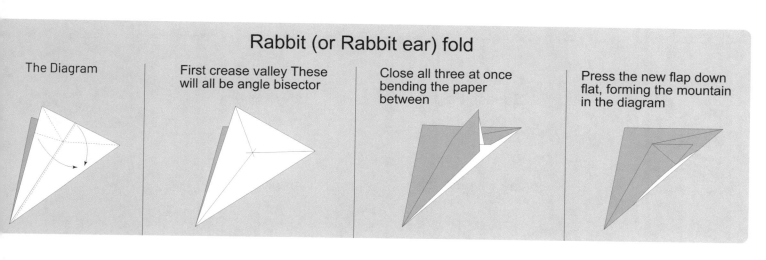

Basic Origami
Symbols

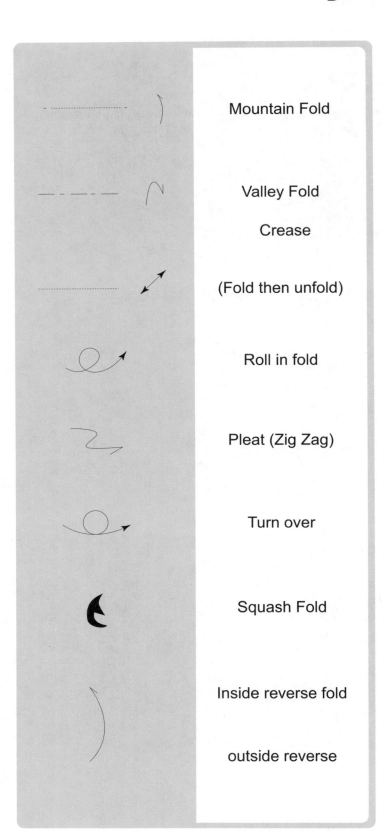

Mountain Fold

Valley Fold

Crease

(Fold then unfold)

Roll in fold

Pleat (Zig Zag)

Turn over

Squash Fold

Inside reverse fold

outside reverse

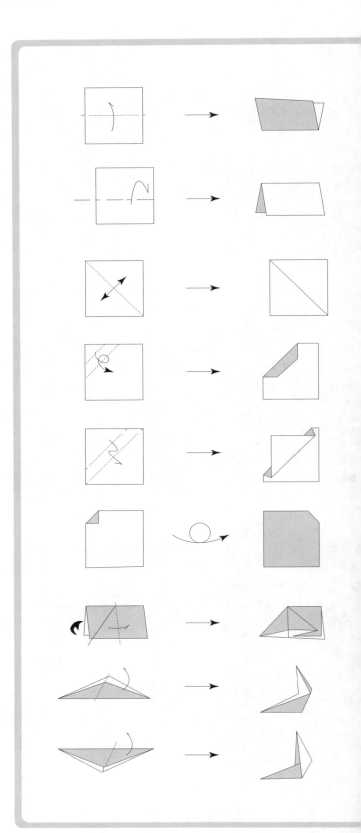

SailBoat

This is a very simple traditional Origami model. The Origami Sailboat makes a perfect decor at a kids party. It can also be used as card embelishment. You could also attach a long thread and use as a garland and hanging display. There are so many possibilities with this easy to remember origami model

SailBoat

Beginner ★ ☆ ☆

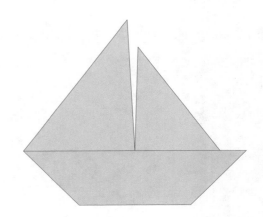

1 Fold in half along the dotted line from bottom and unfold

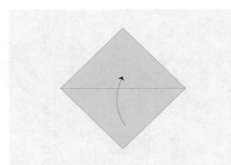

2 Then unfold

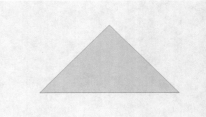

3 Fold the left along the dotted line to the center

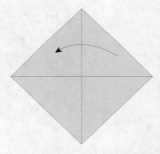

4 Then unfold

5 Fold the left along the dotted line to the center

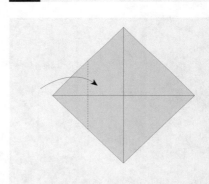

6 Fold the right along the dotted line to the center

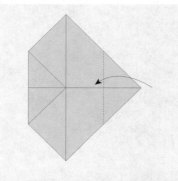

7 Turn 90 degrees

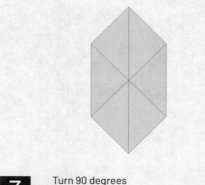

8 Pull the left and right tips up leaving the center point below

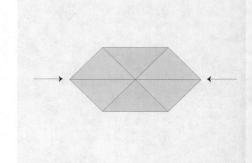

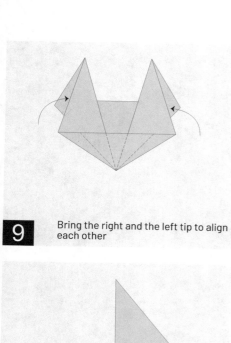

9 Bring the right and the left tip to align each other

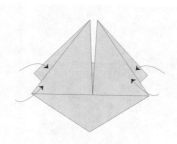

10 Flatten the front and the back flaps

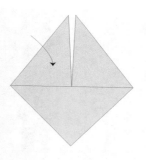

11 Fold the top left flap down

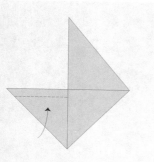

12 Return the front to it's position at the dotted lines

13 Fold the bottom point up in the dotted line

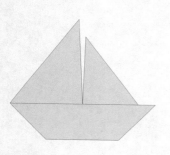

14 Turn over

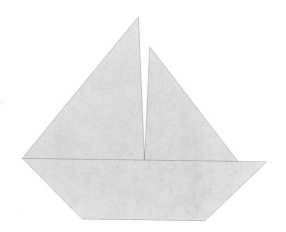

15 Finished!

Cat

Learn how to make Origami cat using craft paper. They can be used as halloween icons. If you are looking for a simple activity in time for the season or you just want to practice your creativity with your favourite animal as the subject, then you will love this instructions for the origami cat.

Cat

Beginner ★

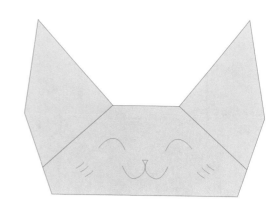

SCAN THIS QR CODE TO WATCH VIDEO INSTRUCTION

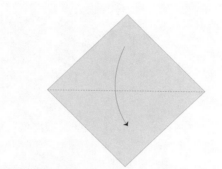

1 Fold in half downward to make a triangle

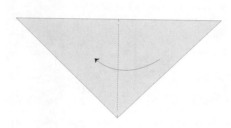

2 Fold in half from left to center to make a smaller triangle

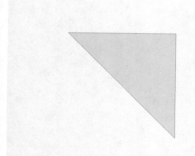

3 Then unfold

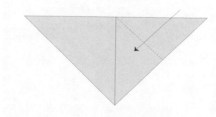

4 Fold the top left corner toward the center

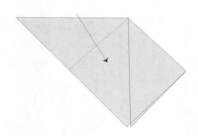

5 Fold the right top corner toward the center

6 Fold the front left flap upward to make the edges hang out

7 Fold the front right flap upward to make the edges hang out

8 Fold the bottom corner upward to align with the top corner

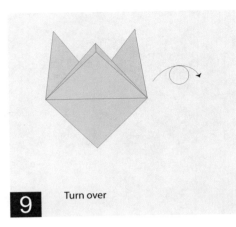

9 Turn over

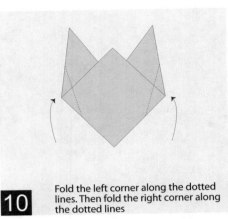

10 Fold the left corner along the dotted lines. Then fold the right corner along the dotted lines

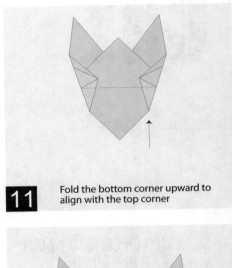

11 Fold the bottom corner upward to align with the top corner

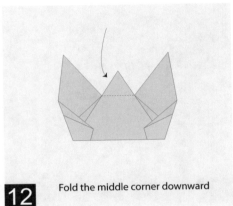

12 Fold the middle corner downward

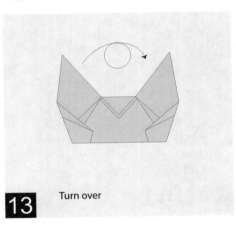

13 Turn over

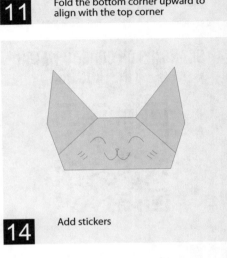

14 Add stickers

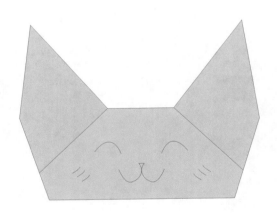

- 18 -

Dove

The Origami dove is a beautiful symbol of peace. The origami is perfect for holidays, weddings and for religious symbolism.

Dove

Beginner ★ ☆ ☆

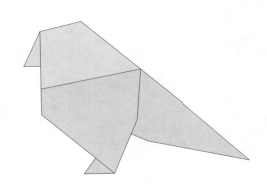

SCAN THIS QR CODE TO WATCH VIDEO INSTRUCTION

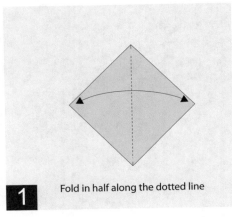

1 Fold in half along the dotted line

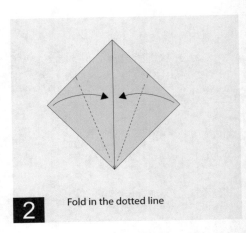

2 Fold in the dotted line

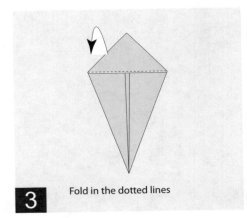

3 Fold in the dotted lines

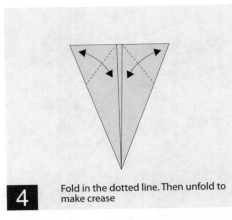

4 Fold in the dotted line. Then unfold to make crease

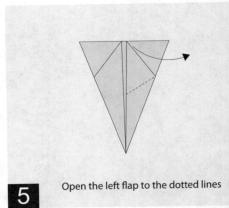

5 Open the left flap to the dotted lines

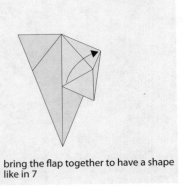

6 bring the flap together to have a shape like in 7

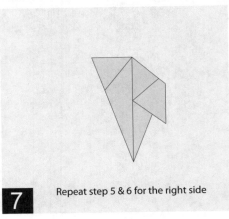

7 Repeat step 5 & 6 for the right side

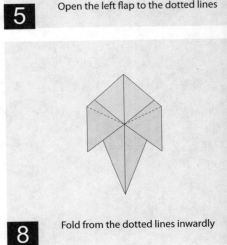

8 Fold from the dotted lines inwardly

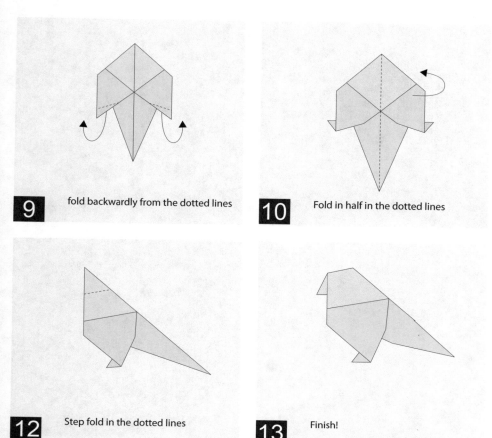

9 fold backwardly from the dotted lines

10 Fold in half in the dotted lines

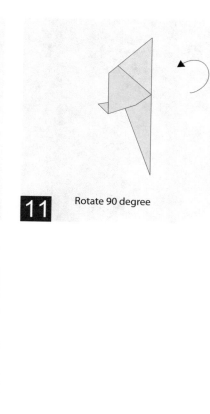

11 Rotate 90 degree

12 Step fold in the dotted lines

13 Finish!

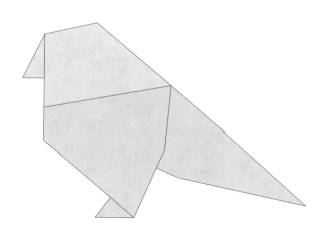

Dog

Keep the kids entertained with this simple origami project to make a colourful paper dog. Fancy folding yourself one of these pocket-sized puppies? Then here is a clear and simple set of instructions showing you are. It is easier than you think with the step by step guide.

Dog

Beginner ★

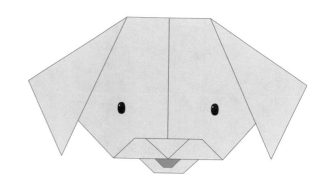

SCAN THIS QR CODE TO WATCH VIDEO INSTRUCTION

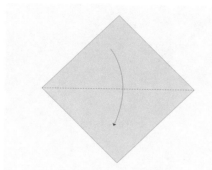

1 Fold in half downward to make a triangle

2 Fold in half sideway to make a smaller triangle then unfold

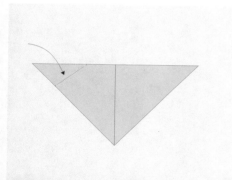

3 Fold down the right corner to make the edges hang out

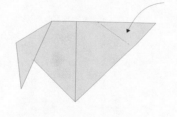

4 Fold down the left corner to make the edges hang out

5 Fold the front bottom corner upward

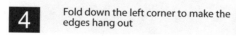

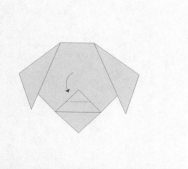

6 From the same triangle, fold the top corner downward

7 Fold the back bottom corner backward

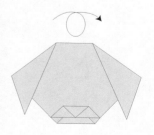

8 Flip over

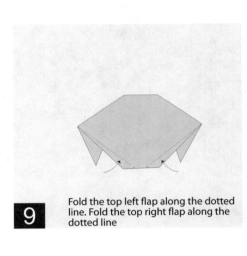

9 Fold the top left flap along the dotted line. Fold the top right flap along the dotted line

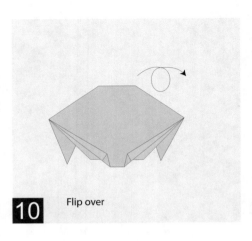

10 Flip over

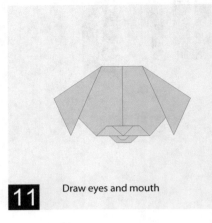

11 Draw eyes and mouth

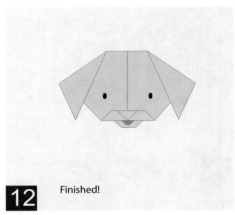

12 Finished!

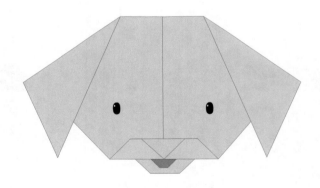

Penguine

These easy origmi instruction will teach you to fold
one using very simple and clear step by step
illustrations. It's so easy that young children can
fold it

Penguine

Beginner  ⭐☆☆

SCAN THIS QR CODE TO WATCH VIDEO INSTRUCTION

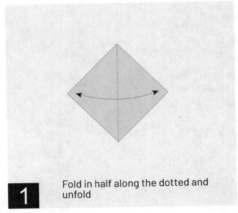

1 Fold in half along the dotted and unfold

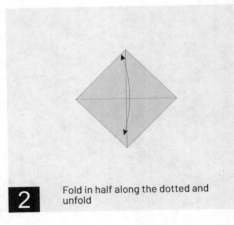

2 Fold in half along the dotted and unfold

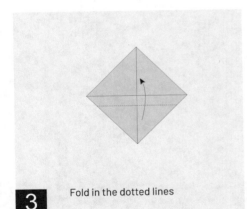

3 Fold in the dotted lines

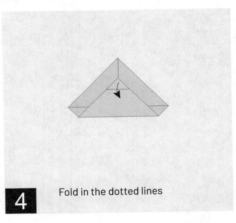

4 Fold in the dotted lines

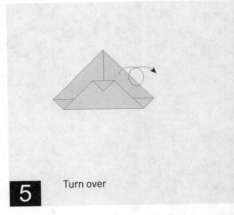

5 Turn over

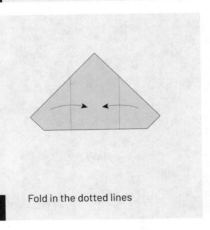

6 Fold in the dotted lines

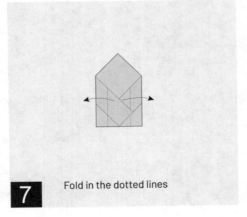

7 Fold in the dotted lines

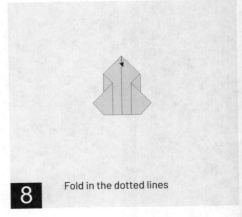

8 Fold in the dotted lines

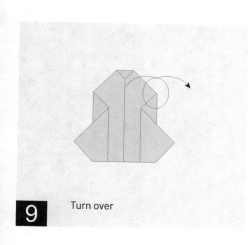

9 Turn over

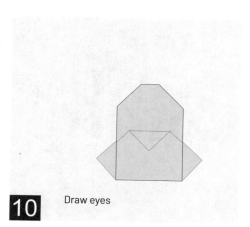

10 Draw eyes

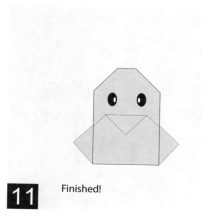

11 Finished!

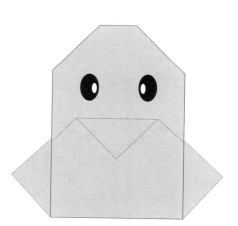

Snake

This origami snake is very easy to fold. Although most people are afraid of snake even though it is one of the most friendly animal, This particular origami snale is very cute. You'll love it.

Snake

Beginner ★

SCAN THIS QR CODE TO WATCH VIDEO INSTRUCTION

1   Fold in half to make crease and unfold

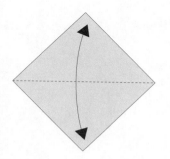

2   Fold in the dotted lines

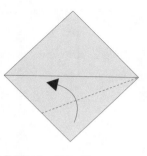

3   Fold in the dotted lines

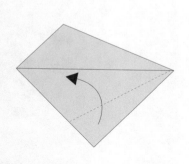

4   Fold in the dotted lines

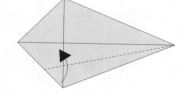

5   Fold in the dotted lines

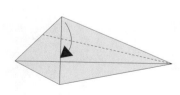

6   Fold in the dotted lines

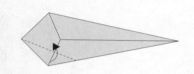

7   Fold in the dotted lines

8   Turn over

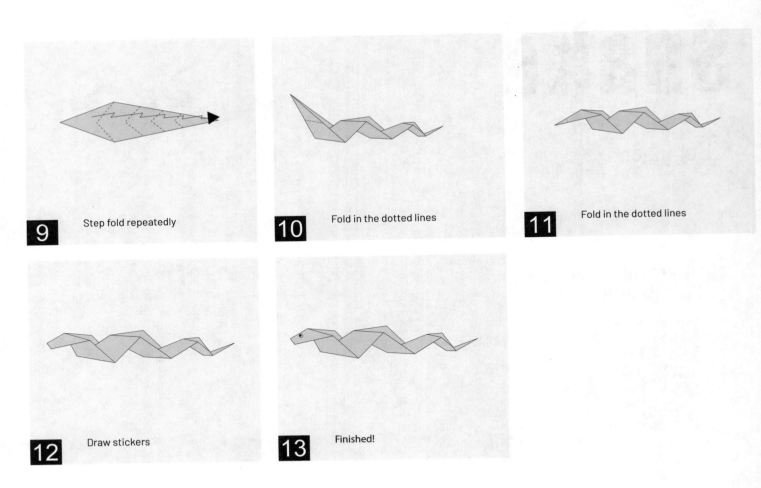

9 Step fold repeatedly

10 Fold in the dotted lines

11 Fold in the dotted lines

12 Draw stickers

13 Finished!

Bird

This origami Bird is a traditional origami design that is easy to make. Just with this simple step, you'll have your origami bird.

Bird

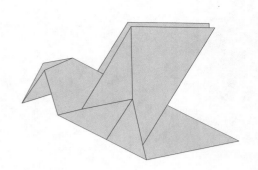

Beginner

SCAN THIS QR CODE TO WATCH VIDEO INSTRUCTION

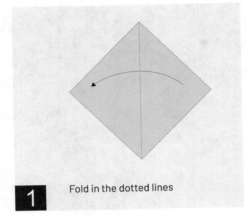

1 Fold in the dotted lines

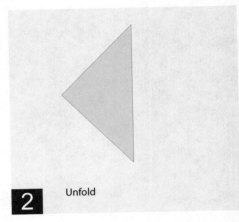

2 Unfold

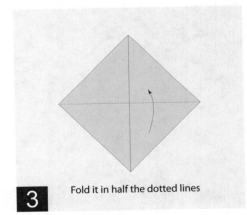

3 Fold it in half the dotted lines

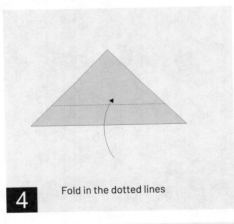

4 Fold in the dotted lines

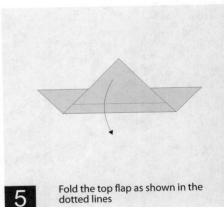

5 Fold the top flap as shown in the dotted lines

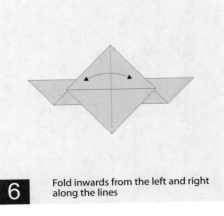

6 Fold inwards from the left and right along the lines

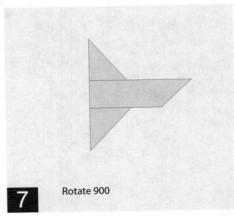

7 Rotate 900

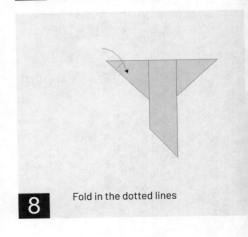

8 Fold in the dotted lines

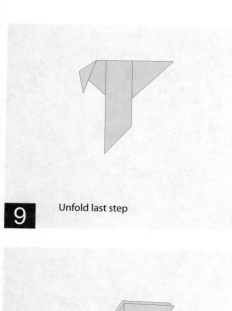

9 Unfold last step

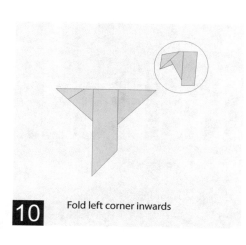

10 Fold left corner inwards

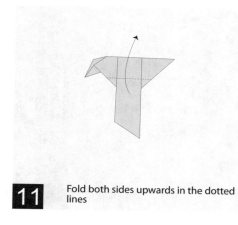

11 Fold both sides upwards in the dotted lines

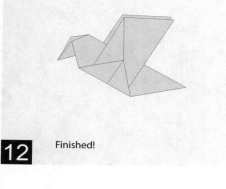

12 Finished!

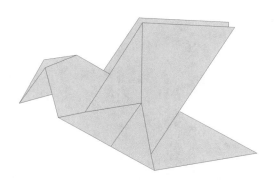

Tulip Flower

Flowers are always beautiful and adorable. So is this origami flower. It's very cute. You can make it for your friend for His party.

Tulip Flower

Beginner

SCAN THIS QR CODE TO WATCH VIDEO INSTRUCTION

1 Fold the upper left corner to the lower right corner, then unfold.

2 Fold the upper right corner to the lower left corner, then unfold.

3 Fold backward, then unfold

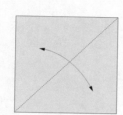

4 Squash fold

5 Fold in the dotted line

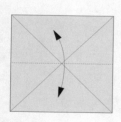

6 Turn Over

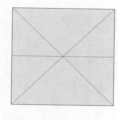

7 Repeat step 5 on this side

8 Open by the center

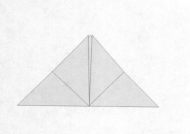

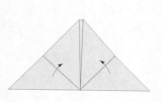

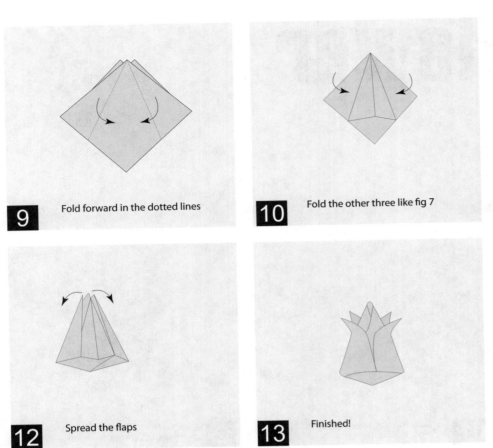

9 Fold forward in the dotted lines

10 Fold the other three like fig 7

11 Blow air in the direction of the arrow

12 Spread the flaps

13 Finished!

Boat

The origami boat is easy to make, and is also a fun action toy. All over the world, the rainy season will many kids building boats. These boat actually float

Boat

Beginner ★ ★ ★

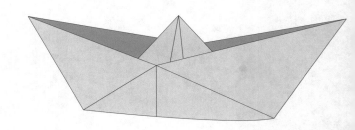

SCAN THIS QR CODE TO WATCH VIDEO INSTRUCTION

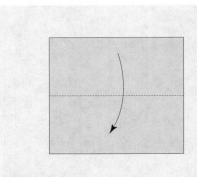

1 Fold in half from the dotted line

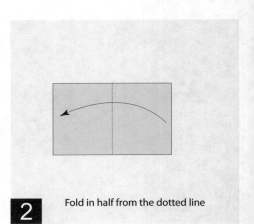

2 Fold in half from the dotted line

3 Then Unfold

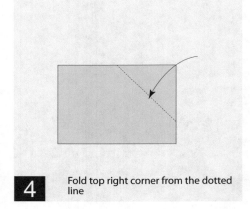

4 Fold top right corner from the dotted line

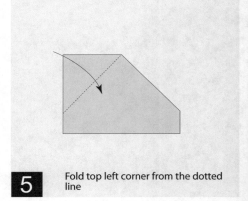

5 Fold top left corner from the dotted line

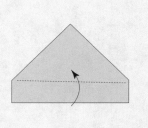

6 Fold upward in the dotted lines

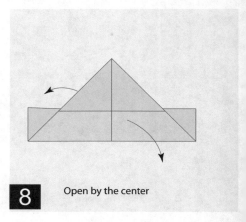

7 Fold inward in the dotted lines

8 Open by the center

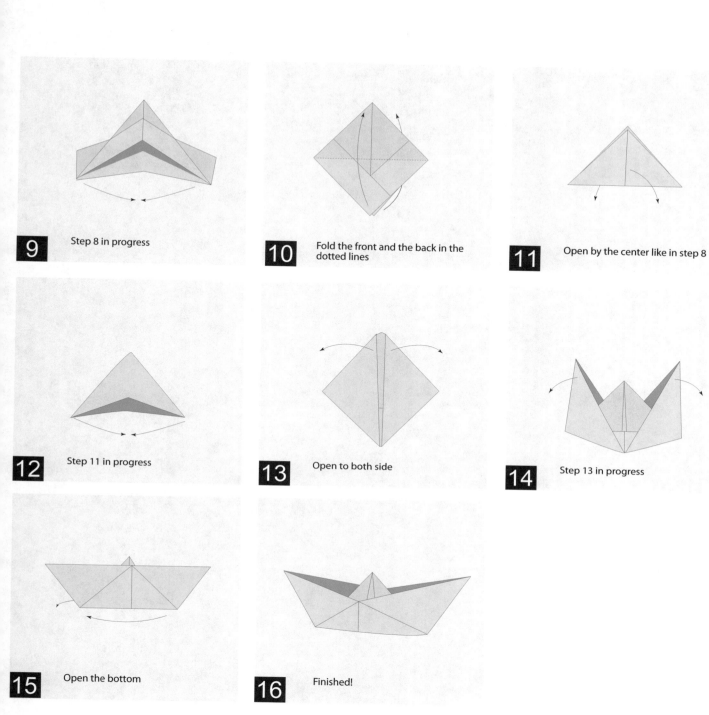

9 Step 8 in progress

10 Fold the front and the back in the dotted lines

11 Open by the center like in step 8

12 Step 11 in progress

13 Open to both side

14 Step 13 in progress

15 Open the bottom

16 Finished!

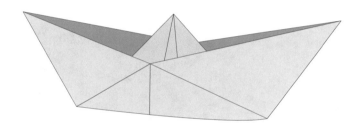

Rectangular Box

This origami box can be used to organise your home office. Instead of buying boxes, why not make it your own as you follow this

Rectangular Box

Beginner ★

SCAN THIS QR CODE TO WATCH VIDEO INSTRUCTION

1 Fold the paper in half diagonally to make creases and unfold.

2 Fold all of the four corners to the central point(marked yellow) to make creases.

3 Unfold the last step

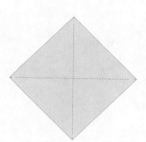

4 Fold from Top(tip) across the dotted lines to make creases and unfold.(The red dot at A meets the red dot at the B). Repeat for C and D. Then unfold

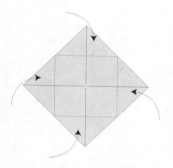

5 Fold from bottom point E inwards to F.

6 Fold from Top point H inwards to G.

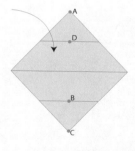

7 Fold inwards from the left and right sides along the dotted lines .

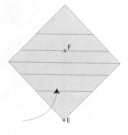

8 Fold inwards from the left and right sides along the dotted lines .

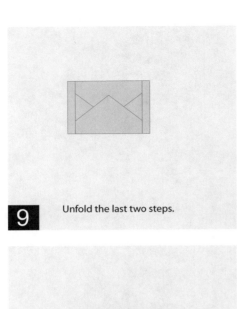

9 Unfold the last two steps.

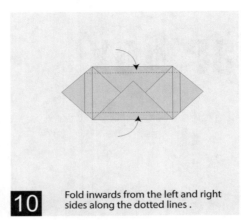

10 Fold inwards from the left and right sides along the dotted lines .

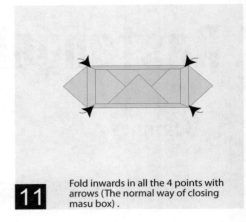

11 Fold inwards in all the 4 points with arrows (The normal way of closing masu box) .

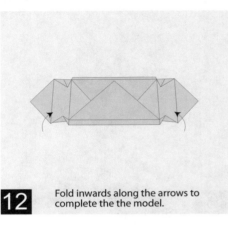

12 Fold inwards along the arrows to complete the the model.

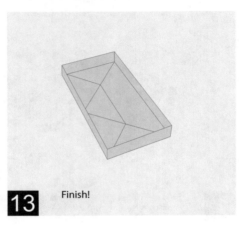

13 Finish!

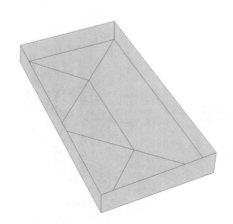

Crown

Origami crown simple origami that can be adjusted
to the size of your head. Have fun!

Crown

Beginner

SCAN THIS QR CODE TO WATCH VIDEO INSTRUCTION

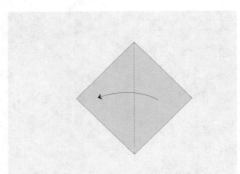

1 Fold to the side and upwards to make creases and a unfold

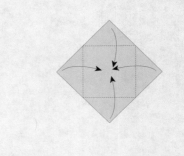

2 Fold all corners into the centre

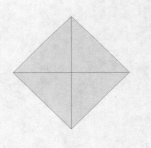

3 Flip the model over

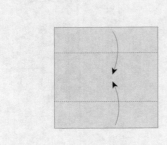

4 Fold the top and bottom toward the centre

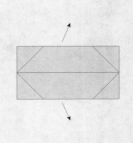

5 Open up the top and bottom flaps

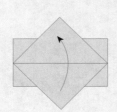

6 Fold the bottom triangle upwards

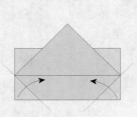

7 Fold the 2 bottom corners upwards

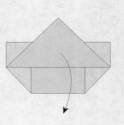

8 Fold the top and bottom toward the centre

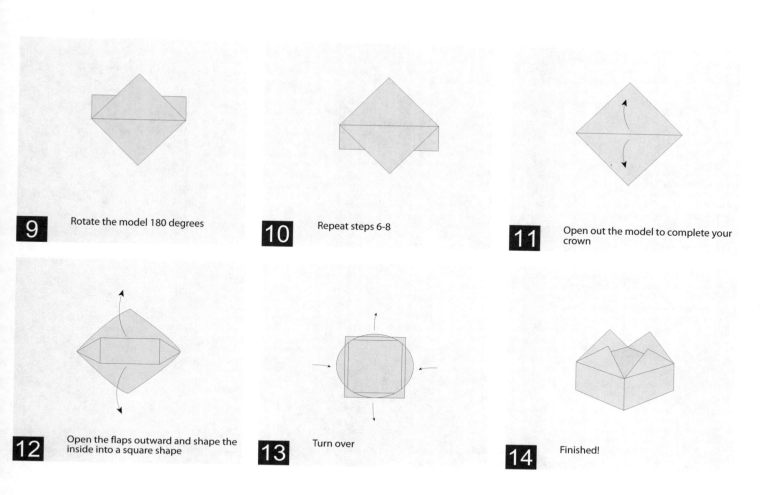

9 Rotate the model 180 degrees

10 Repeat steps 6-8

11 Open out the model to complete your crown

12 Open the flaps outward and shape the inside into a square shape

13 Turn over

14 Finished!

Bat

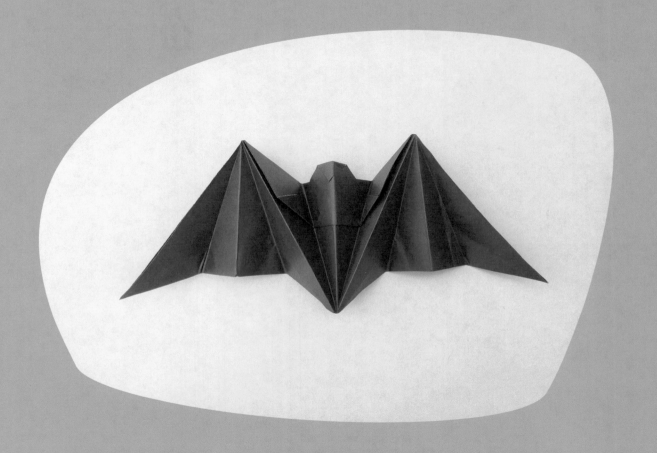

Origami bat makes perfect Halloween decoration. Not only are they easy to fold but they are fantastic hanging up as garland.

Bat

Beginner ★

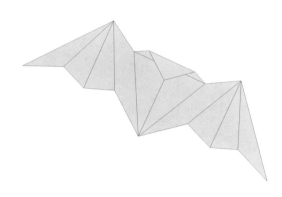

SCAN THIS QR CODE TO WATCH VIDEO INSTRUCTION

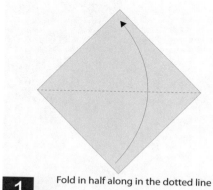

1 Fold in half along in the dotted line

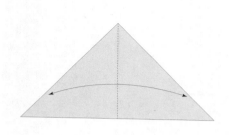

2 Fold the triangle to half and unfold

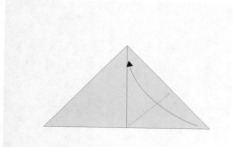

3 Fold the bottom left corner along the dotted line

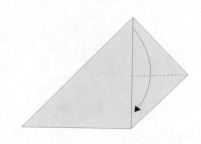

4 Fold down the horizontal edge in half to the bottom diagonal

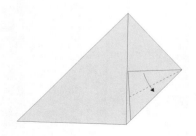

5 Fold in the folded tip in the dotted line

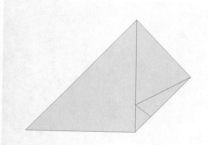

6 Repeat step 3 -5 for the right side of the triangle

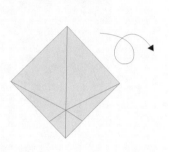

7 Rotate

8 Fold down in half both layers

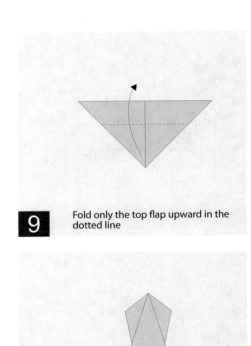

9 Fold only the top flap upward in the dotted line

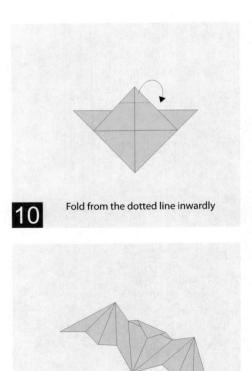

10 Fold from the dotted line inwardly

11 Fold the side edge "a" to the center line "b"

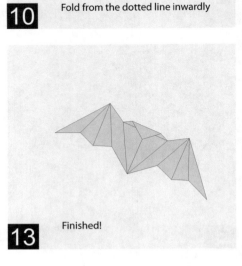

12 Pinch the two point flaps that are inside the layers and pull apart

13 Finished!

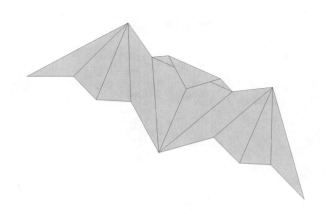

Bee

Everybody loves Bee and this easy origami Bee is no different. After making your own, you can draw on it to picture Bee.

Bee

Beginner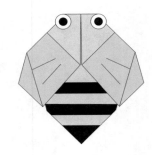

⭐ ⭐ ⭐

SCAN THIS QR CODE TO WATCH VIDEO INSTRUCTION

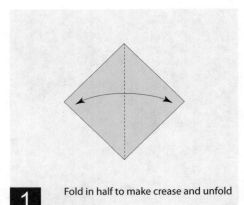

1 Fold in half to make crease and unfold

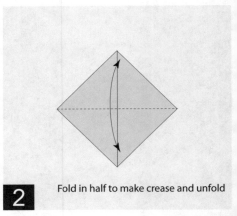

2 Fold in half to make crease and unfold

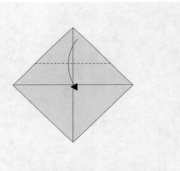

3 Fold in the dotted lines

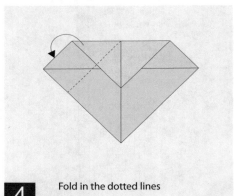

4 Fold in the dotted lines

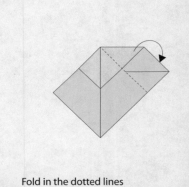

5 Fold in the dotted lines

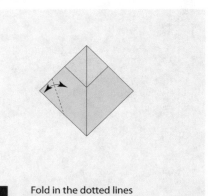

6 Fold in the dotted lines

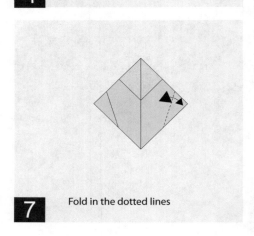

7 Fold in the dotted lines

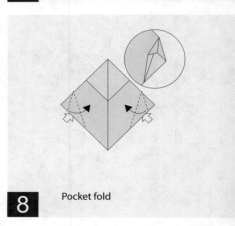

8 Pocket fold

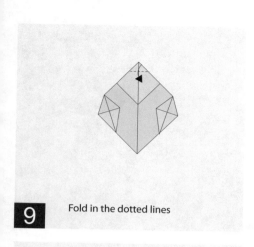

9 Fold in the dotted lines

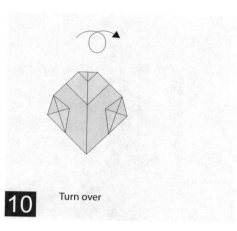

10 Turn over

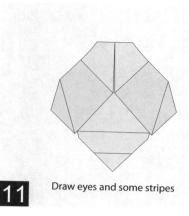

11 Draw eyes and some stripes

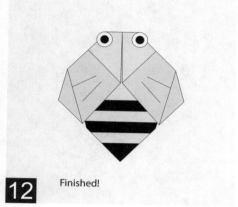

12 Finished!

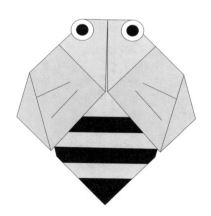

Fish

A pretty origami fish is a cute decoration and a fun way to push your origami skills. This origami is quite easy and only takes a couple of minutes to make. Since it is not too hard to make, it's great for kids to make

Fish

Beginner ★

SCAN THIS QR CODE TO WATCH VIDEO INSTRUCTION

1 Fold in half along the dotted line

2 Then unfold

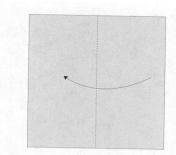

3 Fold the top left and right corners in the dotted lines

4 Fold in the dotted lines

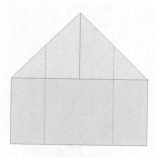

5 Fold the bottom edge up to the top point

6 Fold the bottom left and right corners diagonally up to the top point

7 Unfold the last two steps

8 Result of the previous step

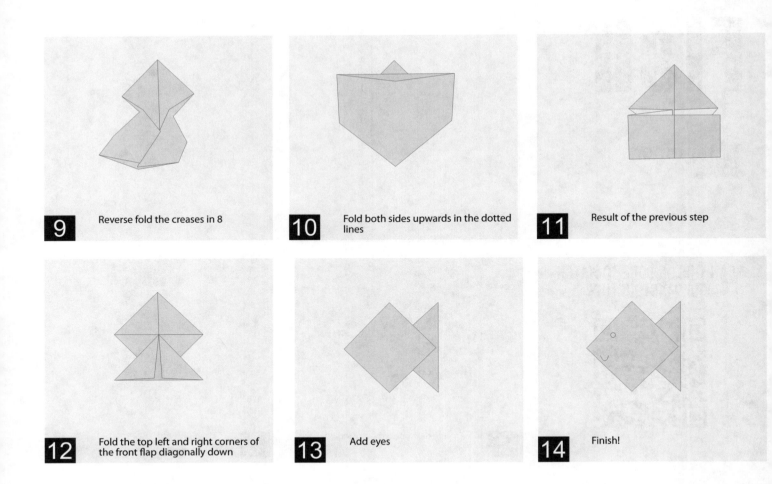

9 Reverse fold the creases in 8

10 Fold both sides upwards in the dotted lines

11 Result of the previous step

12 Fold the top left and right corners of the front flap diagonally down

13 Add eyes

14 Finish!

Elephant Head

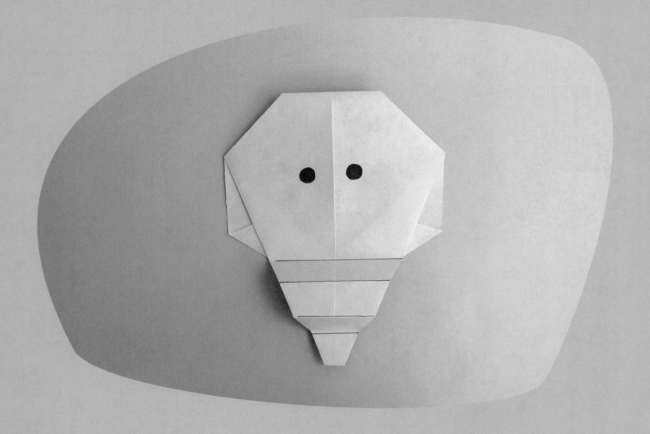

Elephant is one of the most unique animals everyone will want to see. As unique as the animal is, the head is one of the admirable part of the elephant body. It is a simple steps to follow to make the Elephant head.

Elephant Head

Beginner ★ ★ ★

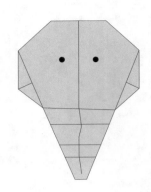

SCAN THIS QR CODE TO WATCH
VIDEO INSTRUCTION

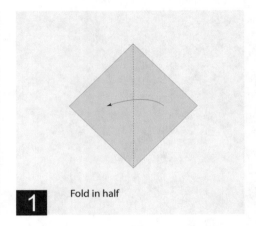

1 Fold in half

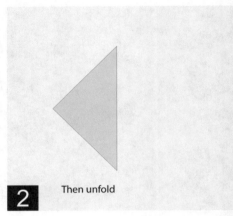

2 Then unfold

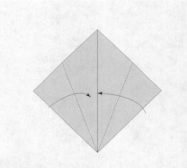

3 Fold the sides from the dotted line to meet the center crease

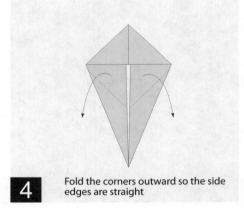

4 Fold the corners outward so the side edges are straight

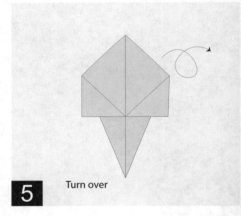

5 Turn over

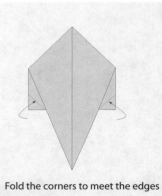

6 Fold the corners to meet the edges

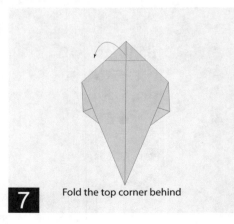

7 Fold the top corner behind

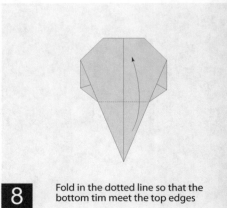

8 Fold in the dotted line so that the bottom tim meet the top edges

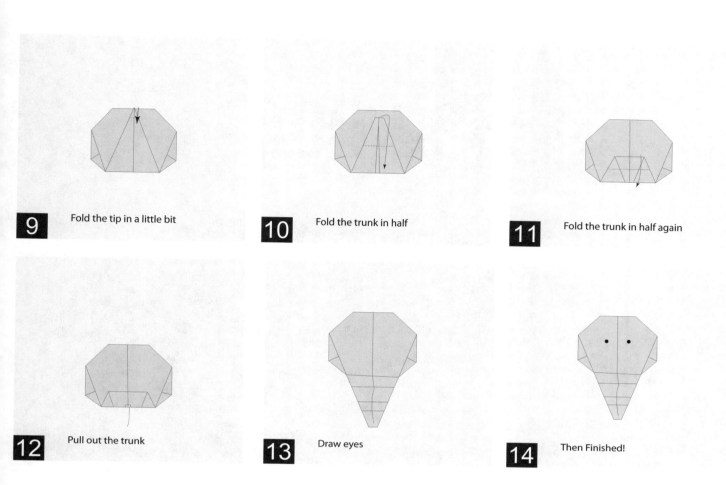

9 Fold the tip in a little bit

10 Fold the trunk in half

11 Fold the trunk in half again

12 Pull out the trunk

13 Draw eyes

14 Then Finished!

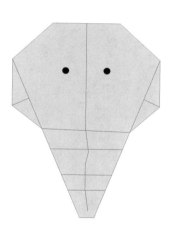

Sea Dog

Sea dog are not the common animals we see around. That's what make the origami intersting because you will always have a type of it in your house.

Sea Dog

Intermediate ★ ★

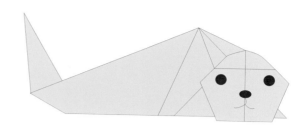

1 Fold in half to make crease and unfold

2 Fold in the top diagonal in the dotted line to meet the center

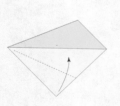

3 Fold in the bottom diagonal in the dotted line to meet the center

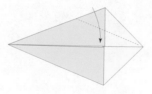

4 Fold in the top diagonal in the dotted line to meet the center

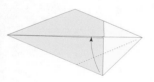

5 Fold in the bottom diagonal in the dotted line to meet the center

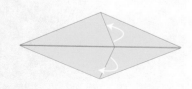

6 Open the   part

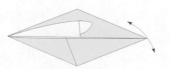

7 Flatten under side

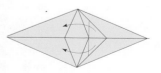

8 Fold in the dotted lines

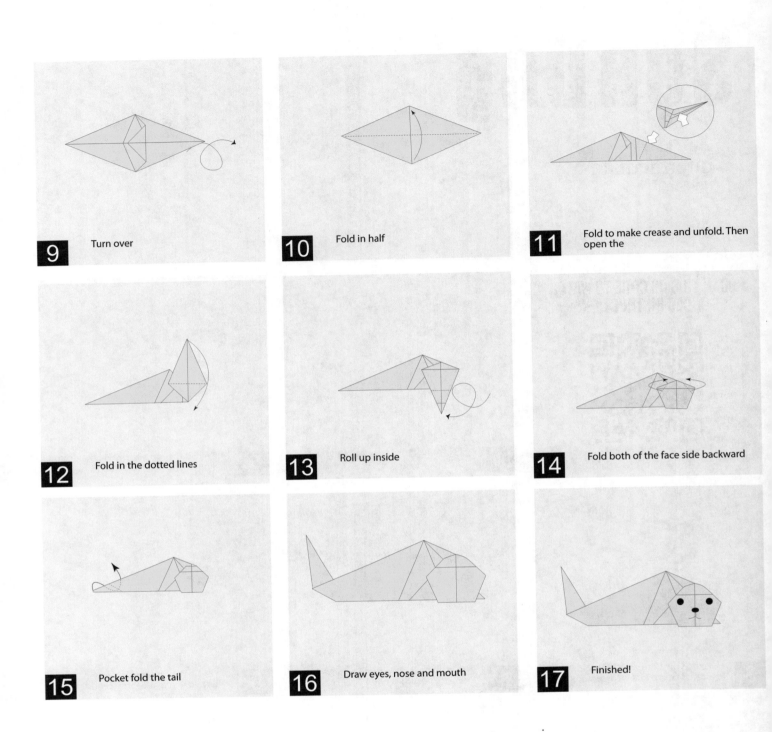

9 Turn over

10 Fold in half

11 Fold to make crease and unfold. Then open the

12 Fold in the dotted lines

13 Roll up inside

14 Fold both of the face side backward

15 Pocket fold the tail

16 Draw eyes, nose and mouth

17 Finished!

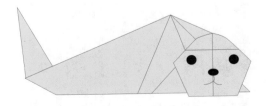

Wild Duck

The following instructions will show how to fols an origami duck. Although for you to be able to do that, you must understand the basic folding techniques.

WildDuck

Intermediate ★ ★ ☆

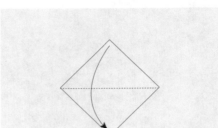

1 Fold in half to make crease and unfold

2 Fold in the top diagonal in the dotted line to meet the center

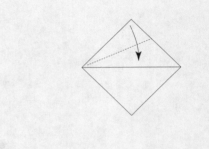

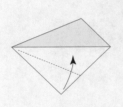

3 Fold in the bottom diagonal in the dotted line to meet the center

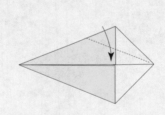

4 Fold in the top diagonal in the dotted line to meet the center

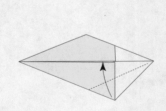

5 Fold in the bottom diagonal in the dotted line to meet the center

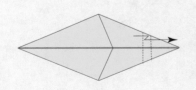

6 Step fold in the dotted lines

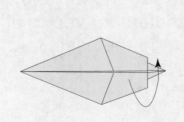

7 Fold in half

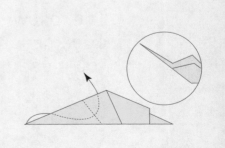

8 Step fold in the dotted lines

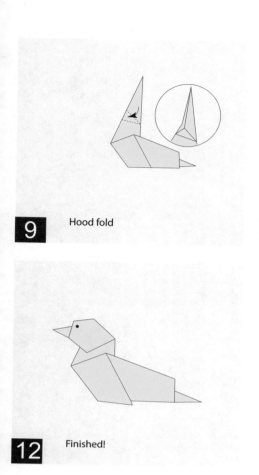

9   Hood fold

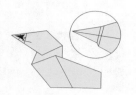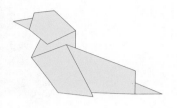

10   Step fold backward

11   Draw eyes

12   Finished!

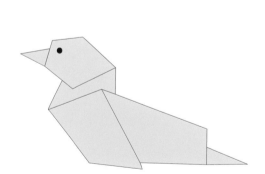

Horse

Origami Horse is one of the most intresting origami you can make. It's not too difficult to make. After you are done, just a sharp tab on the tail and the horse will flip for you.

Horse

Intermediate ★ ★

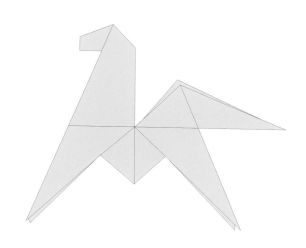

SCAN THIS QR CODE TO WATCH VIDEO INSTRUCTION

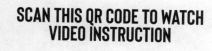

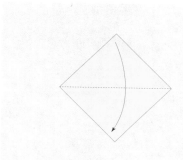

1 Fold in half

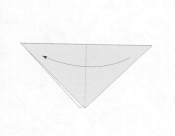

2 Fold in half

3 Open the pocket from 👉

4 Flatten the square

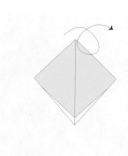

5 Turn over

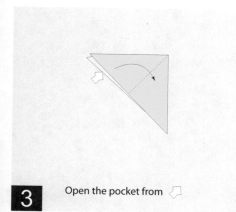

6 Follow the same step as 3 and 4

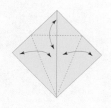

7 Fold the dotted line to make crease

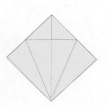

8 Put scissors to the dotted line

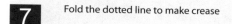

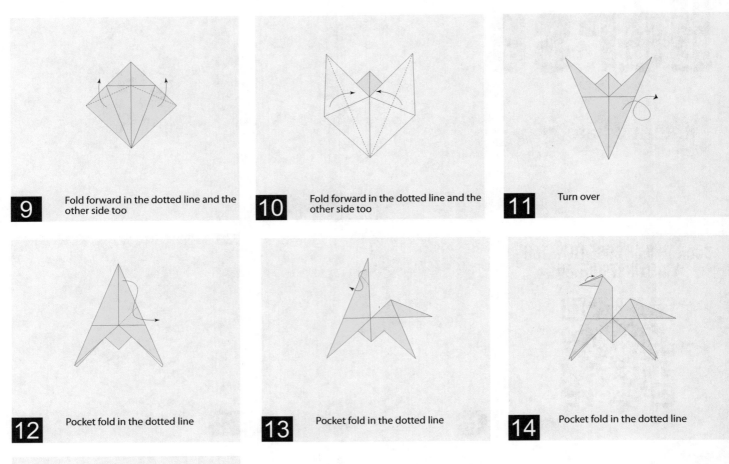

9 Fold forward in the dotted line and the other side too

10 Fold forward in the dotted line and the other side too

11 Turn over

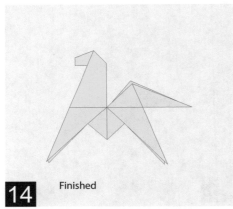

12 Pocket fold in the dotted line

13 Pocket fold in the dotted line

14 Pocket fold in the dotted line

14 Finished

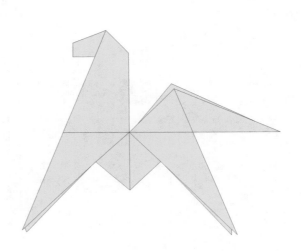

Elephant

Making an elephant is a fun project for anyone experienced in the way of origami. Just follow the instruction step-wisely.

Elephant

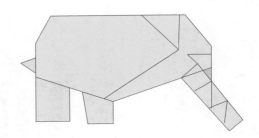

Intermediate

SCAN THIS QR CODE TO WATCH VIDEO INSTRUCTION

1 Fold in all the dotted line

2 Crease left and right front flaps. Repeat on the other side

3 Invert crease made in step two

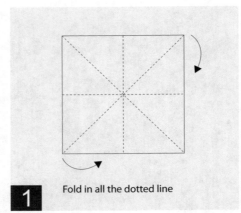

4 Mountain fold top point in half. Then, valley fold bottom front flap upwards

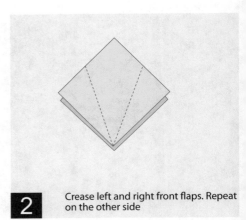

5 inverse fold left and right flaps

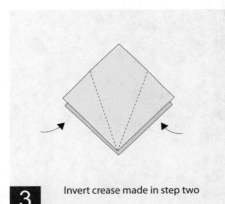

6 fold top front half of right and left flaps upward

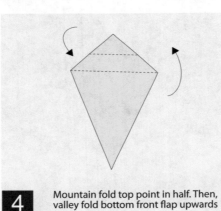

7 Fold right and left points to center

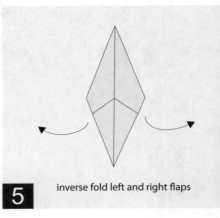

8 Fold right and left arms in half, horizontally along center

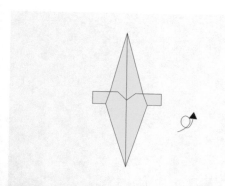

9 Fold entire model in half, and rotate ninety degrees

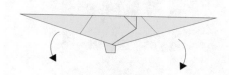

10 Inverse fold right and left sides

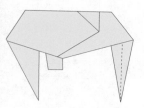

11 Fold the outer edges of the trunk inside, while squash folding top, so points stay sticking out at top

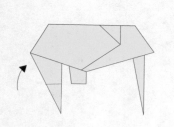

12 Invert hind leg, to be even with front legs. Invert tip, for tail

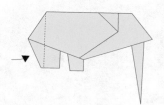

13 Fold in back for hind leg, top and bottom layer

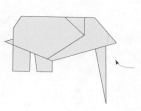

14 Squash fold point above trunk. Repeat on back

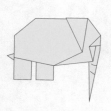

14 With series of inverse folds, pleat the trunk, or otherwise, fold the trunk as desired

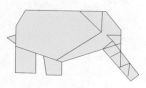

15 Finished!

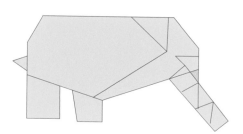

Owl

The origami Owl is a gorgeous piece of paper sculpture. The origami is not too hard for you to male. It is really fun to fold and cool to look at.

Owl

Intermediate ★ ★

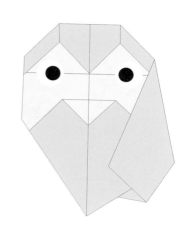

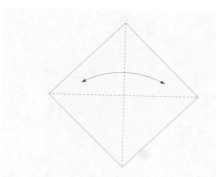

1 fold in half both widthwisely and lengthwisely to make crease

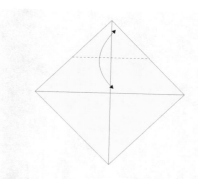

2 Fold in the dotted line. Then unfold to make crease

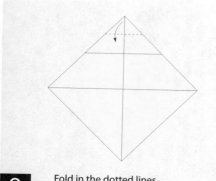

3 Fold in the dotted lines

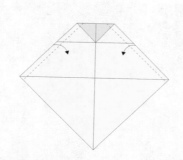

4 Fold the top left and right diagonal in the dotted line

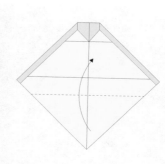

5 Fold from the bottom in the dotted lines

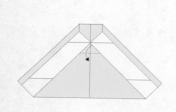

6 Fold the flap down in the dotted lines

7 Fold the dotted line. Then unfold to make crease

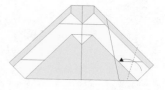

8 Fold in the dotted lines

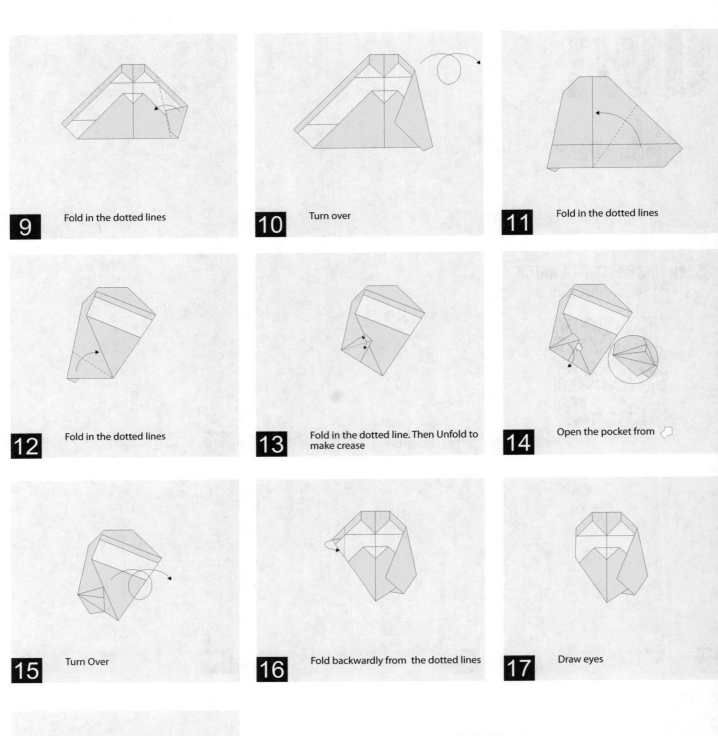

9 Fold in the dotted lines

10 Turn over

11 Fold in the dotted lines

12 Fold in the dotted lines

13 Fold in the dotted line. Then Unfold to make crease

14 Open the pocket from

15 Turn Over

16 Fold backwardly from the dotted lines

17 Draw eyes

18 Finished!

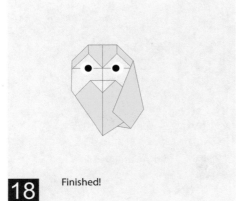

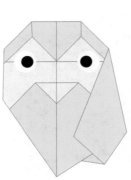

Crab

Learning the origami crab is not too difficult. Just follow the step appropraitely, you will have your Crab. It is cool to see and fun to play with

Crab

Intermediate ★ ★ ☆

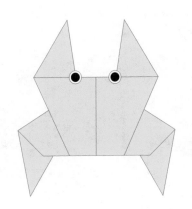

SCAN THIS QR CODE TO WATCH VIDEO INSTRUCTION

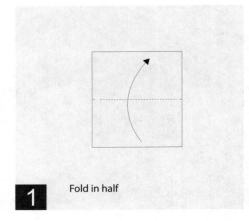

1 Fold in half

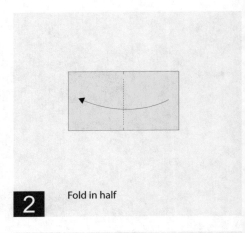

2 Fold in half

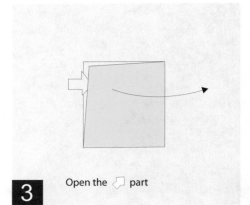

3 Open the 〈 part

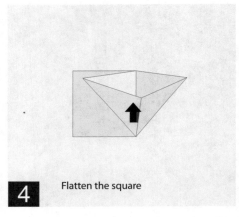

4 Flatten the square

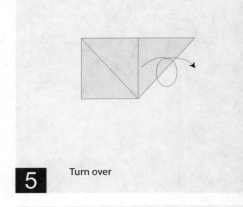

5 Turn over

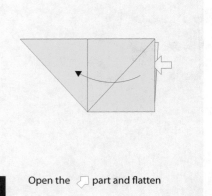

6 Open the 〈 part and flatten

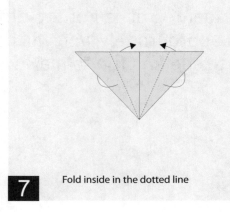

7 Fold inside in the dotted line

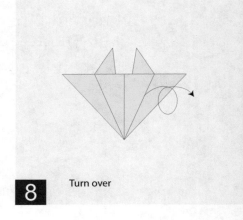

8 Turn over

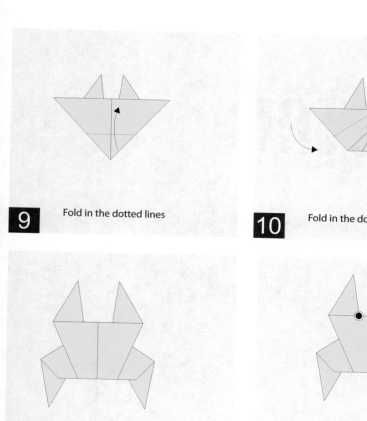

9 Fold in the dotted lines

10 Fold in the dotted lines

11 Turn over

12 Draw eyes

13 Finished!

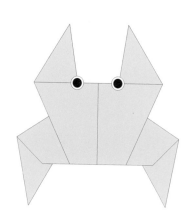

Rooster

Rooster is very symbolic in many culture and religion. This makes it a unique origami you need to learn how to make. The following set of instructions will guide you.

Rooster

Intermediate ★ ★

SCAN THIS QR CODE TO WATCH VIDEO INSTRUCTION

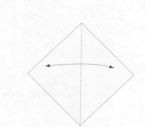

1 Fold in half to make crease and unfold

2 Fold in the left diagonal in the dotted line to meet the center

3 Fold in the right diagonal in the dotted line to meet the center

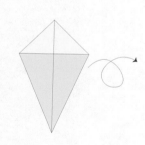

4 Turn over

5 The dots will meet

6 Unfold

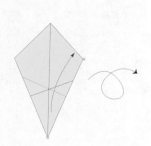

7 The dots will meet and turn over

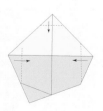

8 Make three valley fold

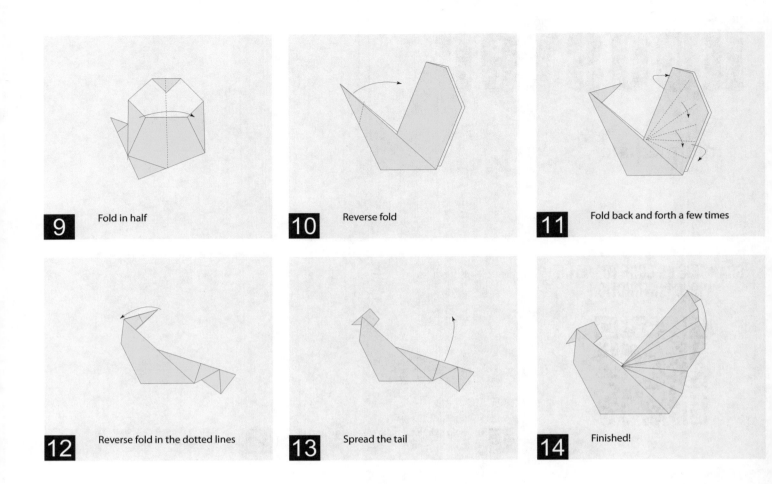

9 Fold in half

10 Reverse fold

11 Fold back and forth a few times

12 Reverse fold in the dotted lines

13 Spread the tail

14 Finished!

Rabbit

This origami Rabbit is quite easy to make if you carefully follow the instructions. Kids will love to make it.

Rabbit

Intermediate ★ ★ ☆

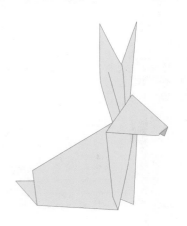

SCAN THIS QR CODE TO WATCH VIDEO INSTRUCTION

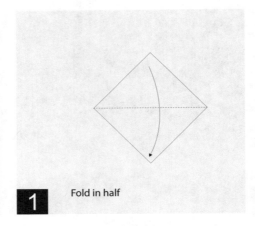

1 Fold in half

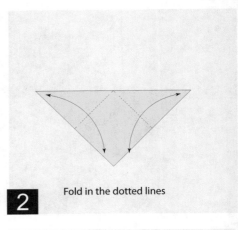

2 Fold in the dotted lines

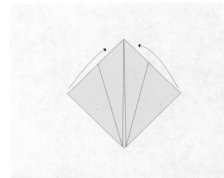

3 Pull up

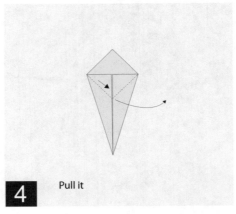

4 Pull it

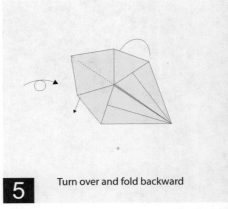

5 Turn over and fold backward

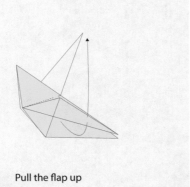

6 Pull the flap up

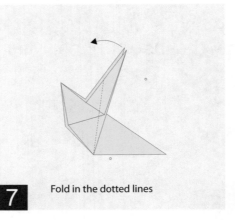

7 Fold in the dotted lines

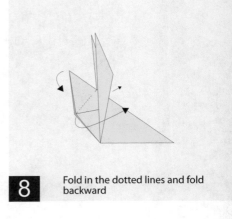

8 Fold in the dotted lines and fold backward

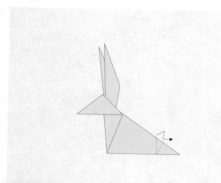

9 Fold in the dotted lines

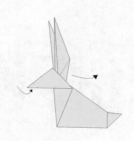

10 Fold in the dotted lines

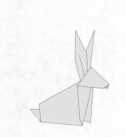

11 Finished!

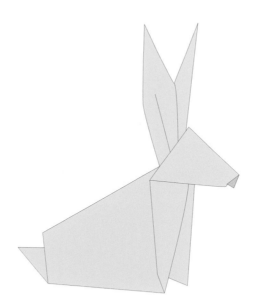

Shark

Shark is an awesome creature. This origami Shark
is beautiful and quite easy to make. You will love it

Shark

Intermediate ★ ★

SCAN THIS QR CODE TO WATCH VIDEO INSTRUCTION

1 Fold in half along in the dotted line

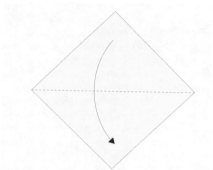

2 Fold in half along in the dotted line

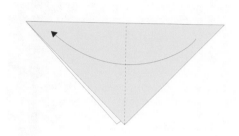

3 Open the pocket from

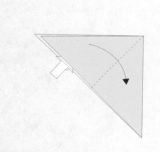

4 Flatten to square

5 Turn Over

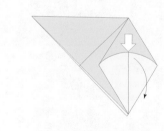

6 Open and flatten the pocket like step 3 and 4

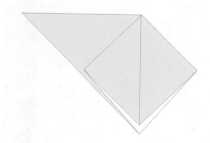

7 Fold to make crease and fold back

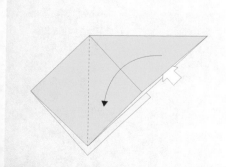

8 Lift to the corner up to make pocket

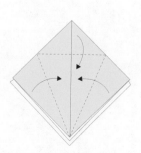

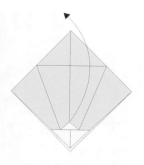

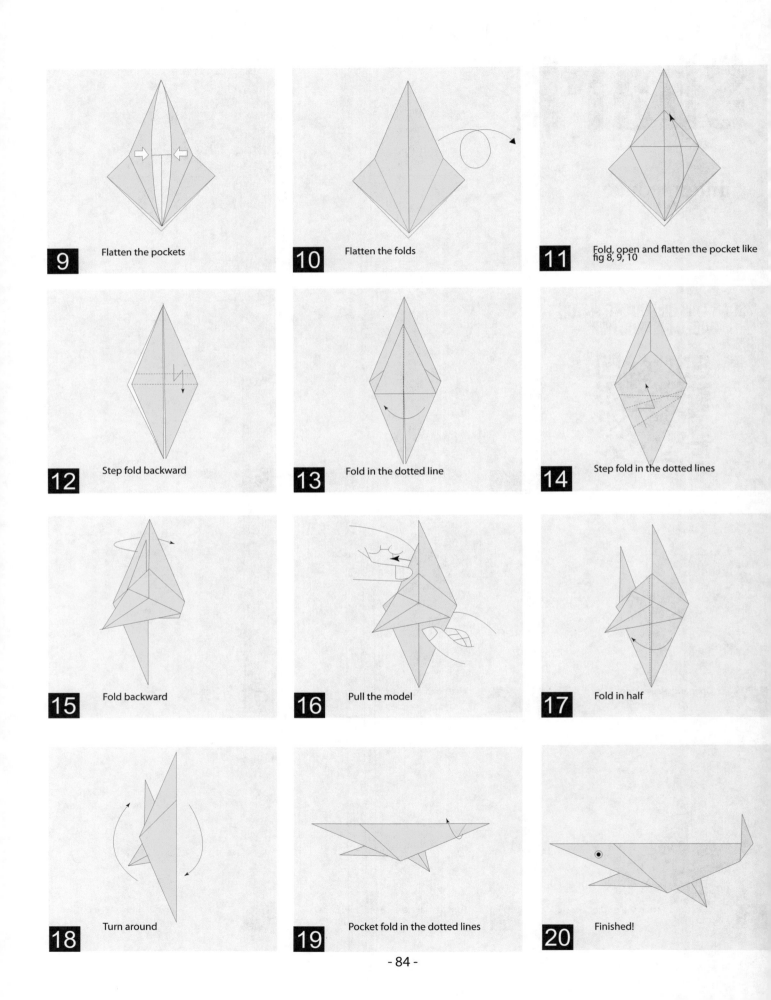

9 Flatten the pockets

10 Flatten the folds

11 Fold, open and flatten the pocket like fig 8, 9, 10

12 Step fold backward

13 Fold in the dotted line

14 Step fold in the dotted lines

15 Fold backward

16 Pull the model

17 Fold in half

18 Turn around

19 Pocket fold in the dotted lines

20 Finished!

Cow

Cows are large, domesticated, cloven-hooved herbivores. The following steps will show you how to make this large animal. Al- though it might seems tricky, but when you follow the instruction well, you will get it right.

Cow

Expert ★ ★ ★

SCAN THIS QR CODE TO WATCH VIDEO INSTRUCTION

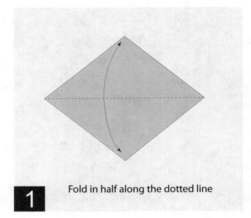

1 Fold in half along the dotted line

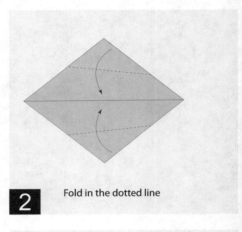

2 Fold in the dotted line

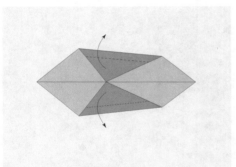

3 Fold in the dotted line

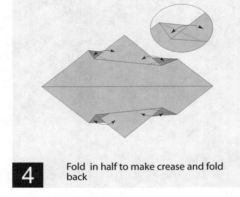

4 Fold in half to make crease and fold back

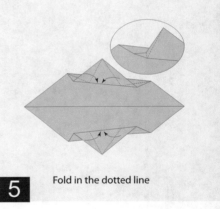

5 Fold in the dotted line

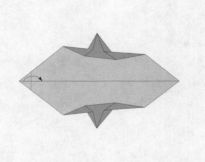

6 Fold in the dotted line

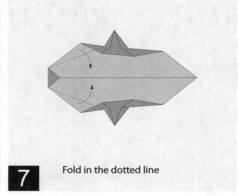

7 Fold in the dotted line

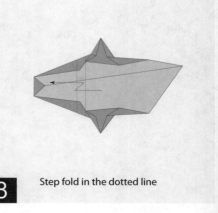

8 Step fold in the dotted line

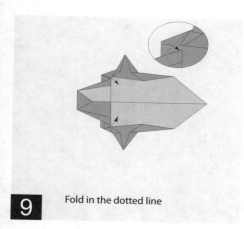

9 Fold in the dotted line

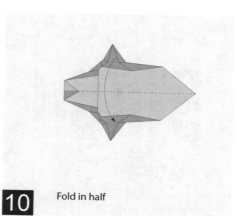

10 Fold in half

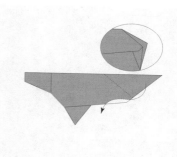

11 Pocket fold

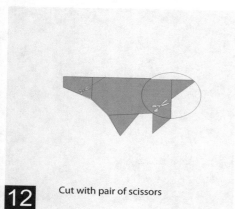

12 Cut with pair of scissors

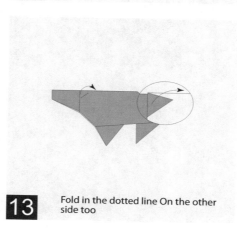

13 Fold in the dotted line On the other side too

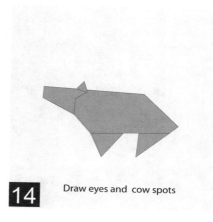

14 Draw eyes and cow spots

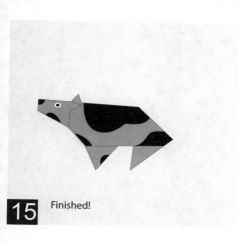

15 Finished!

Squid

Squid are cephalopods with elongated bodies. This make it a unique origami to make. Although it's difficult to make, but it will looks simple after you completed your first model when you follow tthe instruction thoroughly

Squid

Expert ★ ★ ★

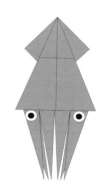

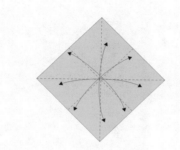

1 Fold in halves in the dotted line to make crease

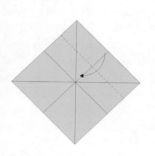

2 Fold in the dotted line

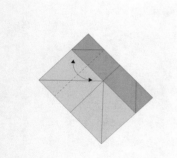

3 Fold to make crease and fold back

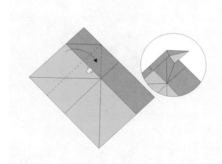

4 Open the ↻ part and flatten

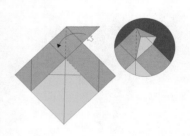

5 Open the ↻ part and flatten

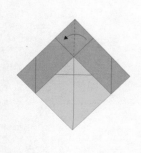

6 Fold in the dotted line

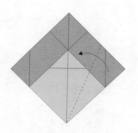

7 Fold in the dotted line

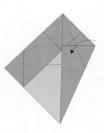

8 Fold in the dotted line

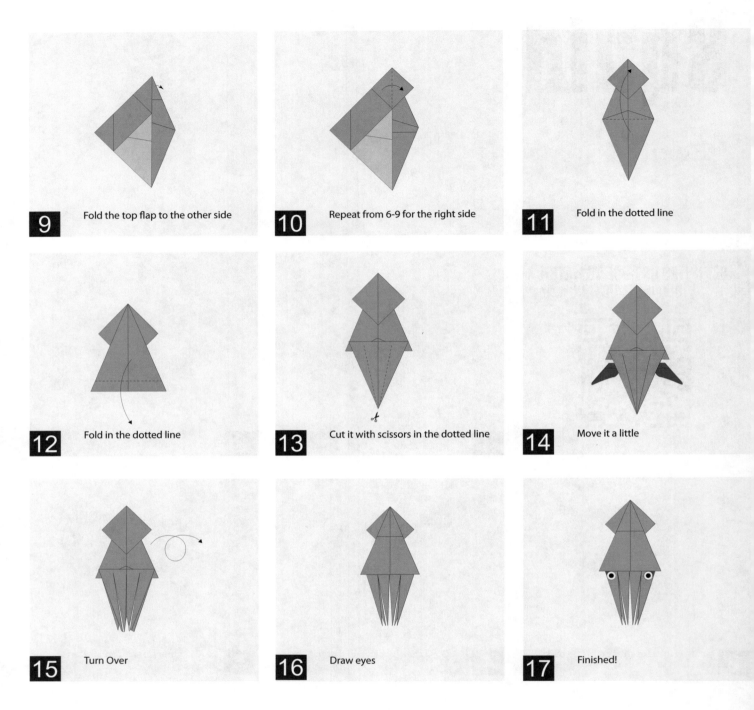

9 Fold the top flap to the other side	**10** Repeat from 6-9 for the right side	**11** Fold in the dotted line
12 Fold in the dotted line	**13** Cut it with scissors in the dotted line	**14** Move it a little
15 Turn Over	**16** Draw eyes	**17** Finished!

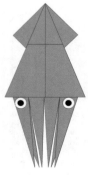

Grasshoper

Origami grasshopper is not a super easy origami to make. Nonetheless, the instructions are simple enough for you to be able to make your own. The grasshopper is insect children love to see. This makes it a model you will want to have.

Grasshoper

Expert ★ ★ ★

1 Fold in half from the dotted line

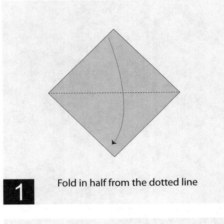

2 Fold in half from the dotted line

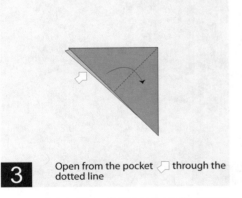

3 Open from the pocket ⬜ through the dotted line

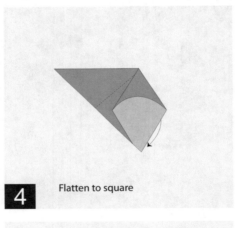

4 Flatten to square

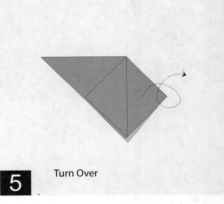

5 Turn Over

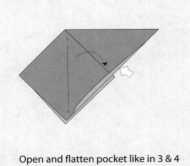

6 Open and flatten pocket like in 3 & 4

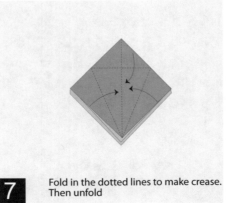

7 Fold in the dotted lines to make crease. Then unfold

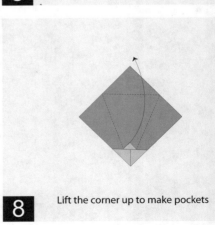

8 Lift the corner up to make pockets

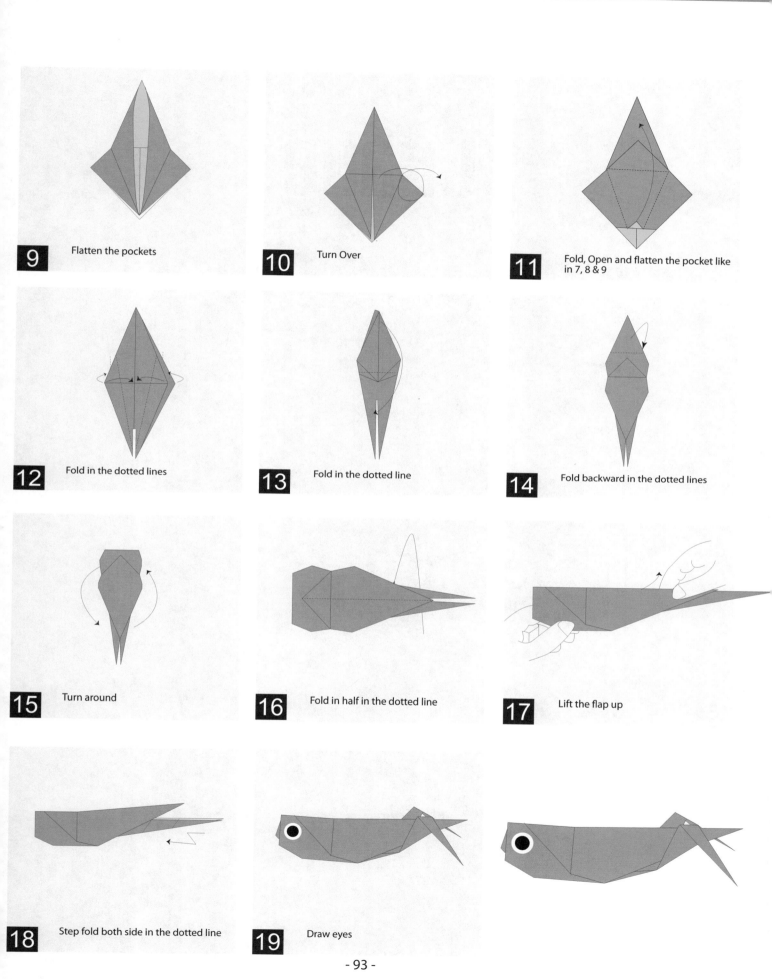

9 Flatten the pockets

10 Turn Over

11 Fold, Open and flatten the pocket like in 7, 8 & 9

12 Fold in the dotted lines

13 Fold in the dotted line

14 Fold backward in the dotted lines

15 Turn around

16 Fold in half in the dotted line

17 Lift the flap up

18 Step fold both side in the dotted line

19 Draw eyes

Crane

The crane is quite difficult to make especially if you
don't have proper knowlege of folding. Notheless,
as you follow this step by step instruction, you will
be able to make the crane as easy as possible.

Crane

Expert ★ ★ ★

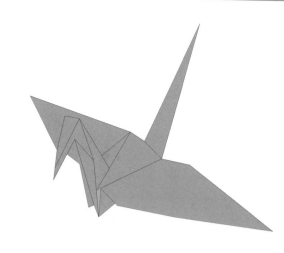

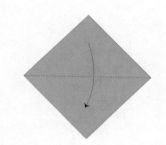

1 Fold in half along the dotted line

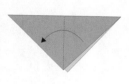

2 Fold in half from right to left diagonally again

3 Spread the pocket out from the inside and fold to make a small square

4 Result from previous step

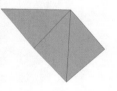

5 Your paper should look like this. Now turn it over to start step six

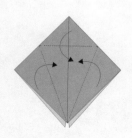

6 Fold left and right corner to center line. Also Fold top corner down to center line

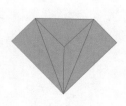

7 Your paper should look like this

8 Now, open the pocket by pulling the buttom corner up and fold inward along the crease. Some creases will become inverted

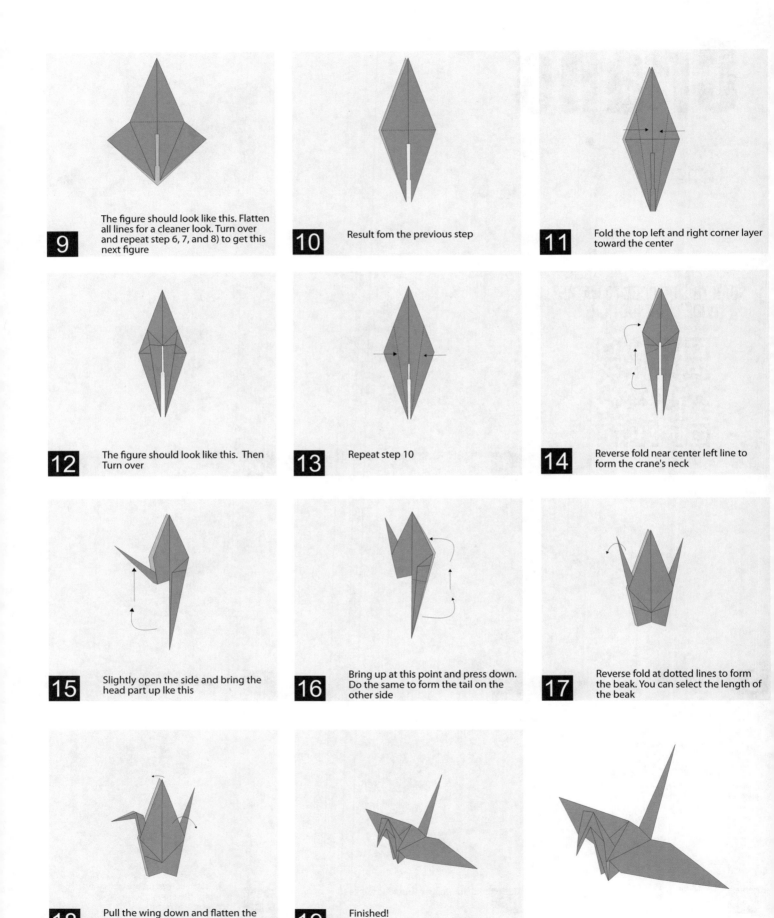

9 The figure should look like this. Flatten all lines for a cleaner look. Turn over and repeat step 6, 7, and 8) to get this next figure

10 Result fom the previous step

11 Fold the top left and right corner layer toward the center

12 The figure should look like this. Then Turn over

13 Repeat step 10

14 Reverse fold near center left line to form the crane's neck

15 Slightly open the side and bring the head part up lke this

16 Bring up at this point and press down. Do the same to form the tail on the other side

17 Reverse fold at dotted lines to form the beak. You can select the length of the beak

18 Pull the wing down and flatten the body into a square

19 Finished!

Frog

These easy to follow instructions will show you how to fold tradi- tional origami jumping frog. This origami frog can actually jump pretty far if you press down on its back!

Frog

Expert ★ ★ ★

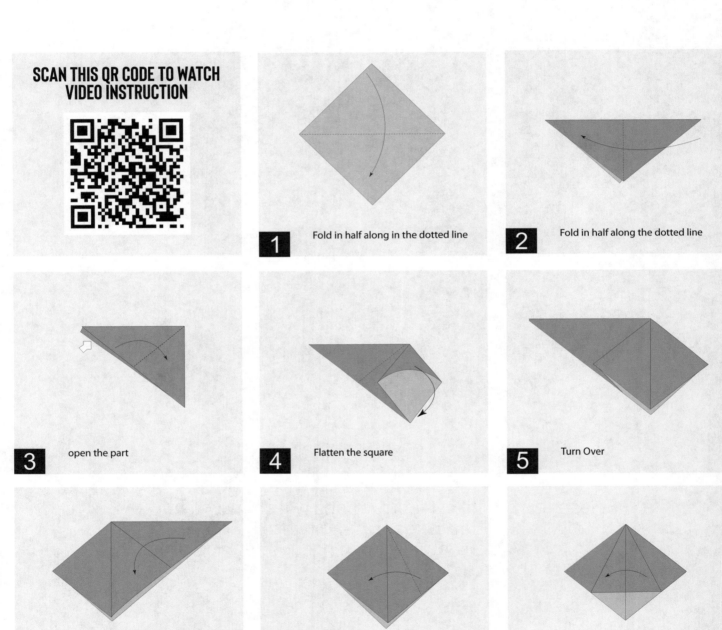

1 Fold in half along in the dotted line

2 Fold in half along the dotted line

3 open the part

4 Flatten the square

5 Turn Over

6 Follow the same step as 3 and 4

7 Fold in the dotted line

8 Fold others in the dotted line

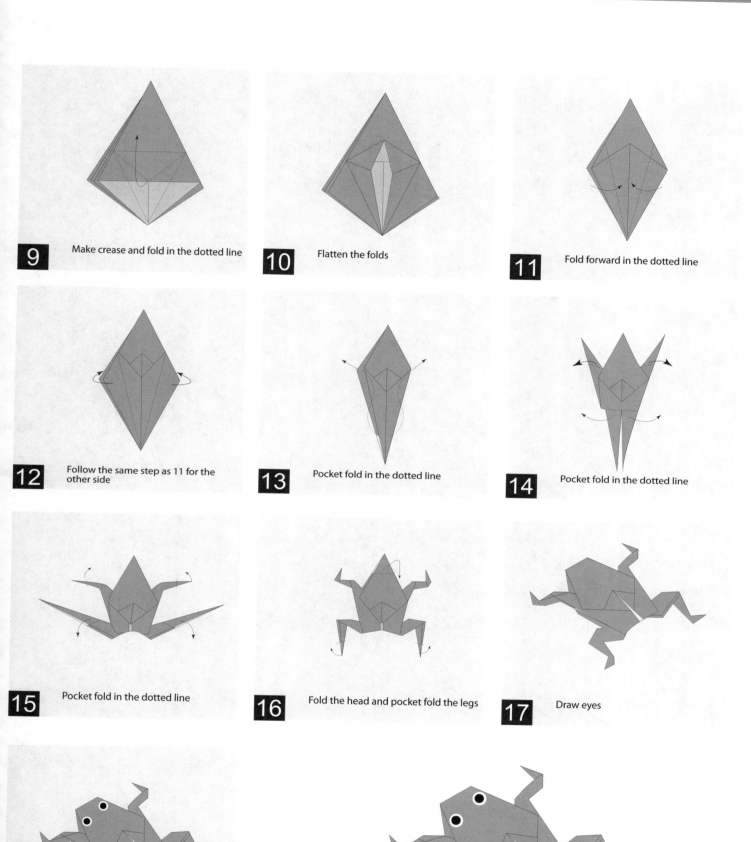

9 Make crease and fold in the dotted line

10 Flatten the folds

11 Fold forward in the dotted line

12 Follow the same step as 11 for the other side

13 Pocket fold in the dotted line

14 Pocket fold in the dotted line

15 Pocket fold in the dotted line

16 Fold the head and pocket fold the legs

17 Draw eyes

18 Finished!

Turtle

When it comes to riddles, turtle takes the first stage. This make it a unique origami everyone will want to make. Al- though it's quite difficult, but following the step, you will get the model

Turtle

Expert ★ ★ ★

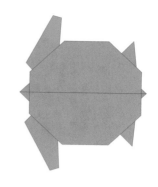

1 Fold in half along in the dotted line

2 Fold in half along in the dotted line

3 Open the pocket from ▱

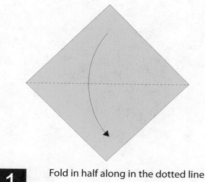

4 Flatten to square

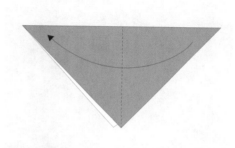

5 Turn Over

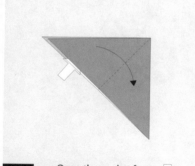

6 Open and flatten the pocket like step 3 and 4

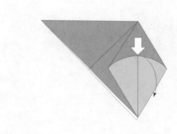

7 Fold to make crease and fold back

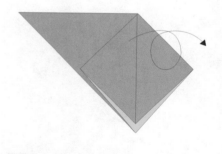

8 Lift to the corner up to make pocket

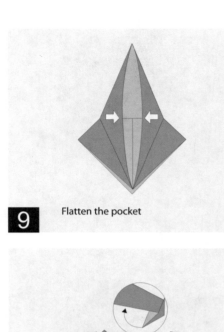

9 Flatten the pocket

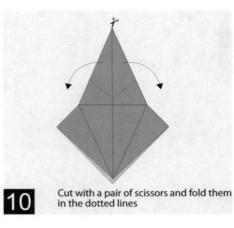

10 Cut with a pair of scissors and fold them in the dotted lines

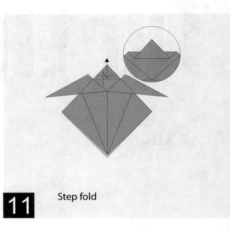

11 Step fold

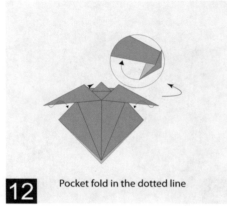

12 Pocket fold in the dotted line

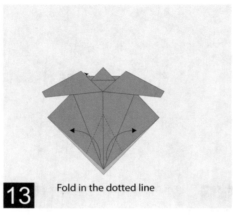

13 Fold in the dotted line

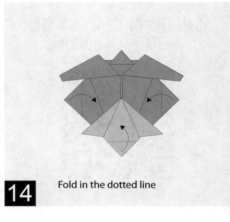

14 Fold in the dotted line

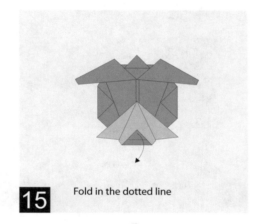

15 Fold in the dotted line

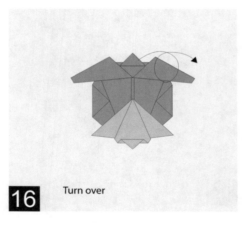

16 Turn over

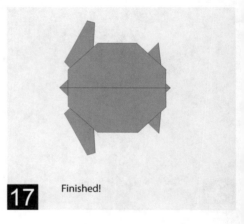

17 Finished!

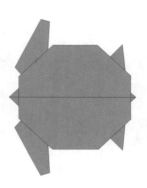

Made in United States
Troutdale, OR
12/20/2024

27103896R00058